ABOUT THE AUTHOR

PAUL FOSTER was born in Salem, New Jersey, and graduated from Rutgers. Aside from *Tom Paine,* he has written four one-act plays, *Balls, The Recluse, Hurrah for the Bridge,* and *The Hessian Corporal,* which will also be published by Grove Press. All the plays were produced in repertory by the La Mama Troupe when it toured Europe in the summer of 1967. Foster has just finished working on an experimental television show for NET, and holds a Rockefeller Foundation Grant. He is at work on his first film and on a new play.

EVERGREEN PLAYSCRIPT
No. 21

Consulting editor:
Henry Popkin

Evergreen Playscript Series

TOM PAINE

a play in two parts

by Paul Foster

Grove Press, Inc.

New York

Library of Congress Catalog Card Number: 68-22021

First Printing

Manufactured in the United States of America

This play is dedicated
to the La Mama (E.T.C.)
Experimental Theater
Club Troupe

Acknowledgments:

Edgar Negret, the sculptor, who gave me the copy of
Common Sense which incited the play.

Dr. Paul Cranefield, who researched books, documents,
unpublished letters, journals, notes, and maps and
ferreted out every one of Tom Paine's addresses
on our Sunday walking tours and who piled all this
information in a neat stack . . . so I
could throw it all away and begin to write a play.

Ellen Stewart, of the La Mama Experimental Theater
Club, who every week rings a handbell and announces,
"Good evening, ladies and gentlemen,
welcome to Café La Mama, dedicated to the playwright
and all aspects of the theater". . . She means it.

INTRODUCTION

I am trying to remember what it was first like to read the script of *Tom Paine*. Of course, my senses are not virgin to the plays of Paul Foster, having directed all but one of his plays in one medium or another, so it is impossible for me to get to where your innocence may be. But the thought of the reader having to crack the script unforewarned is somewhat disturbing.

The play was developed conjointly with the La Mama Troupe and myself, as director. Because of or in spite of this, it took us several months to understand this highly inventive play. The terrain of Foster's work is not easy to know. His theater impulses seem to spring from earlier times and are mixed with new invention; they bear little relationship to the recent past; they never impose a secondary reality, but instead deal directly with the confrontation of the audience and the play.

Choice and chance have always played a large part in art, whether it has been in interpretations or in procedure, and in the current theater, choice and chance have recently been reinstated in a place of dignity. In *Tom Paine,* Foster has explored more deeply into this territory than he has in his other plays, and the sense of chance operates more fully. By offering the actors improvisational "seed lines" which are to be planted in a body of improvised moments, and initiating freely improvised discussion of the play, in which, in our production, the audiences were encouraged to participate, the audience is presented with three levels of theatrical reality: The level of the text, which is tightly set down by the author to be performed exactly as written. The improvisational level, which freely uses the seed lines. And the third level of open discussion.

Another example of the audience's choice comes with Foster's view of the protagonist. In all of his plays, with the exception of *The Hessian Corporal*, Foster has purposely chosen as hero a character who is beyond empathy. In *Hurrah for the Bridge*, Rover is a thoroughly destroyed man making his last journey. *The Recluse* is a fragmented old woman scrounging through the rubble of our society. In *Balls*, the two heroes are even more remote—they are abstracted as two swinging ping-pong balls. In *Tom Paine*, the audience is further distanced, not only by Foster's choosing the controversial character of Paine, who was at once one of our greatest heroes and made by some into an archvillain, but by his dividing the personality into a real self and a reputation. This inaccessibility works inversely, forcing audiences to fill the vacuum where the nature of the traditional theatrical hero usually is. The result is profoundly disturbing.

Further choice is required of the audience by the presentation of both facts and fallacies, and by the lack of time sequence. In the scenes of the Crossing to America, time and occurrences have been telescoped and invented: the thirty-seven-year-old Paine appears simultaneously as a sixteen-year-old street boy and a man in his deathbed agonies. The audience is bombarded with fragments and details of fact with subjective coloration. The viewer comes away with a subliminal residue which he has culled for himself.

8

For a director, the play presents the widest horizon of possibilities. More than in Foster's other plays—and most other works I have been associated with—images are allowed a kaleidoscopic freedom. Foster has come up with poetic ideas which require theatrical ingenuity on a par with *Peer Gynt* and *The Tempest*. And if some people felt our production was too richly produced, only a cursory glance at the script's requirements is necessary to realize that we even fell short of what is there.

Perhaps future productions can bring to the stage some of these images: I still do not know how to represent on stage a herd of turtles with burning candles on their backs and make them disappear as instantly as they appeared. But this is the adventure of working with a powerfully imaginative script.

The world of Paul Foster's theater is a highly contemporary one, fragmented, burning hot and cold, offering data and facts, noncommital, without solutions: The audience is made to feel the urgency of responsibility.

—Tom O'Horgan

Part One of this play was first performed in May, 1967, at the La Mama (E.T.C.) Experimental Theater Club, New York, by the La Mama Troupe, with sets designed by Kikuo Saito, lights designed by Laura Rambaldi, and costumes designed by Michael Warren Powell and Helen Rostagno. In addition to those listed below, the cast also included Seth Allen, Blanche Dee, and Shellie Feldman.

The entire play was first performed at the Edinburgh International Festival, September, 1967, in the Church Hill Theatre, under the auspices of the Traverse Theatre, with the following cast from the La Mama Troupe:

PART ONE

John Bakos: Tom Paine's Reputation
Mari-Claire Charba: 1st Deaf Woman, The American Committee of Secret Correspondence, A Greedy, The Woman in the Red Cloak
Peter Craig: Major Domo, Roger
Jerry Cunliffe: Sergeant, Captain, General, Quartermaster, Gouverneur Morris, King George III of England
Claris Erickson: Gin Seller, 2nd Deaf Woman, A British Spy, A Greedy
Kevin O'Connor: Tom Paine
Victor LiPari: Private, Mate, Drummer, Silas Deane
Beth Porter: Beulah, A Greedy, Count de Vergennes
Michael Warren Powell: Bishop, Caron de Beaumarchais
Marilyn Roberts: Marie; John Jay, President of Congress; A Greedy
Rob Thirkield: Altar Boy, Quaker, Old Man, Governor, Black Dick, King Louis XVI of France

11

PART TWO

John Bakos: Tom Paine's Reputation

Mari-Claire Charba: Marguerite Bonville

Peter Craig: Major Domo

Jerry Cunliffe: Burke, Sentry, Sergeant, King George III of England

Claris Erickson: Mary Wollstonecraft, Old Man, 2nd Registrar

Kevin O'Connor: Tom Paine

Victor LiPari: The Shadow of Cromwell, Private, Sentry, Drummer, The Lord Justice

Beth Porter: Simonne, 1st Registrar

Michael Warren Powell: Barrister Horsely, Captain Lambesc

Marilyn Roberts: Queen Marie Antoinette, Marie

Rob Thirkield: Blake, King Louis XVI of France

A Chorus of Greedies. A Chorus of Children. Winds and Waves.

Set designer: Hamish Henderson
Light designer: André Tammes
Stage manager: Steve Whitson
Company manager: Bill Muir

The second performance of the entire play took place at the Vaudeville Theatre, London, in October, 1967, with the La Mama Troupe. Lights designed by Francis Reid, produced by Michael White.

12

The play was first performed in the United States by the La Mama Troupe at the Stage 73 Theater, New York, in March, 1968, produced by William Dorr. Lights designed by John Dodd, costumes designed by Michael Warren Powell, and stage manager, Steve Whitson. Cast also included Michael Miller and Sally Kirkland.

DIRECTOR AND MUSIC COMPOSER
FOR ALL PRODUCTIONS:

TOM O'HORGAN

TOM PAINE

SCENES IN PART ONE:

Time: 1809

Place: A bear pit, Lower Manhattan

Cast: An ensemble of twelve actors who play a variety of parts regardless of gender. The lines not assigned to a particular actor may be spoken by anyone, as appropriate.

Basic Costume: Black—knickers, jerseys, skirts, leotards, ballet shoes.

PART ONE

Exercise your twitches, itches, limps, blinks, waddles. Specific characters begin to take shape imperceptibly and at different times.

A large barn with bales of hay, overhead hoist rope, a large rocking affair to one side that looks generic to this place.

As audience enters, actors casually bring in your own props, improvise lines about each other, your props, their locations, bus connections, etc. Seed improvisation lines with following lines on a rotational basis, a different actor each night in chance form:

If this is a bear pit, why all this hay?

They eat it.

EAT IT?!

They had strange diets in 1809.

The bears sleep on it.

GOGOL THE GIANT! (*Hisses.*) He was the favorite.

AND KASHA! (*Cheers.*) Not as big, but twice as quick.

Anybody seen the drum?

It's on my hump.

Help me with my fingernails.

A harpsichord is placed center. The actor who plays PAINE *tunes a note. Everyone tune. Sit at small stools around him. Begin to play crumhorns, oboes, recorders, cymbals, serpent, triangle. Play GIN, GIN, GIN song, while conversation and lines continue. Make yourselves comfortable, a weird Baroque chamber concert.*

What are those birds who pick up shiny things?

Crows.

Magpies.

Oh, come on. *This* is the barn.

A bear pit.

All right, this is the bear pit. Lower Manhattan. 1809.

(*Indicate beyond.*) There the bears. Outside, both armies slaughter each other. And in here . . . well . . .

In here another sport.

In here the fugitives.

The frayed leftovers, pick over the trappings like crows.

Like magpies.

Like *crows*!

Attracted by anything that shines.

Where's the drum?

Are they almost seated now?

I think so.

Carry harpsichord to side. Continue to play other instruments.

Group, form crawling centipede, still singing song. Then, one by one, stand, advance and present yourself to audience. State your own name, clear, proud, stately, and bow, saying each a line:

Tom Paine came from Thetford, England.

His father was a bastard.

His father made corsets.

He went to London. That pest hole.

He was 37 when he left.

He was exiled.

He was *not exiled*!

He went with a letter of recommendation from Benjamin Franklin.

And he bade his friends good-by.

His friends were Goldsmith and the mystic Blake.

And he made the great crossing to America.

And he lived in a bear pit in New York.

Immediately: Two put on soldiers' hats and get rifles. PRIVATE *drum a sharp roll. Silence. Talk and badger these two at will.*

SERGEANT: TOM PAINE, wanted for sedition and treason, whose whereabouts are known to be in this vicinity of Five Points. All persons having information are ordered to step forth. A reward will be given. By order, General Burgoyne, Commander of this here district. All right, Private, search this wallow! Gawd, it stinks. Never knew a place to stink up so bad.

Group, unified animal growling.

PRIVATE: What's that?!

SERGEANT: Bears.

PRIVATE: BEARS! Gawd, I ain't enlisted to tackle no bears.

SERGEANT: They're chained, Private. They make 'em fight. And they bet on the winner. Got it? Now search.

PAINE actor, from hay, grab his ankle.

PRIVATE: AHH! HE'S GOT ME!

SERGEANT: All right, now what's your name, lovely?

A wretched human, fingernails unbelievably long, hair matted to his head, dirt encrusted. Slobbering gutteral animal grunts.

PRIVATE: He sounds like one of them animals.

SERGEANT: Hey, you, on your feet.

ACTOR OF PAINE: Gimme drink. (*Fall over.*)

PRIVATE: I . . . I think he's dead.

SERGEANT: I think he's drunk. All right, keep it moving, Private. On your post. We'll just wait. (*Pace.*) Is this some duty for a FULL sergeant? I could have been stationed at Government House tonight. No. What do I get?

PRIVATE: Five Points.

SERGEANT: The asshole of New York.

PRIVATE: Of the world. (*Pace.*) Sergeant, what's he look like? I mean, how will we know we got him, if we get him?

SERGEANT: By his eyes. He's got the eyes of the Devil. He stirred up this whole mucking war. The General knows him, knows him by sight, and that's why nobody leaves till the General gets here.

PRIVATE: Gawd, it stinks.

Improvise comments on bear pit, then on Marie's costume, as MARIE, *a large woman, enters.*

FEMALE: Marie enters and throws her weight around.

MARIE: All right. Pay up or sleep out in the snow. Nobody sleeps in my barn without cash.

Complain.

MALE: Now the Sergeant throws his weight around. He is clearly outmatched.

SERGEANT: Hold on. Hold on!

He cannot get attention. PRIVATE *roll drum. Quiet for a second.*

That's better. Nobody goes no place.

MARIE: You're generous with my hotel, Sergeant. Who's going to pay?

SEVERAL: The Sergeant pays.

SERGEANT: Hotel? This place ain't fittin' for animals.

ALL (*angrily*): Not fittin' for animals. You heard the Sergeant. Nobody pays.

MARIE: Then everybody sleeps out in the snow.

Complain. Drum roll. Pick him up and carry him around.

PRIVATE: TOM PAINE, wanted for sedition and treason, whose whereabouts are known to be in this vicinity of Five Points. All persons having information are ordered to step forth. A reward will be given. By order, General Burgoyne, Commander of this here district.

BISHOP (*addled and simple*): I know him. I KNOW HIM!

SERGEANT: Is that the truth?

MARIE: Anything's possible.

BISHOP: He used to sleep in my corner over there.

MARIE: It's an in and out business, Sergeant.

SERGEANT: Is he here now?

MARIE: Sergeant, we're honest people. Look at us. We'd never betray one of our own. At least not for the scrawny price you're offering.

BISHOP (*yelp up and down*): I know him!

SERGEANT: What's the matter with him?

Gag BISHOP. *Get him into corner. Begin to dress him in ratty* BISHOP *robe.*

MALE: He's strange.

FEMALE: Marie made him sleep out in the snow, and he got "frostbit" in the head.

One ask if you can *get frostbit in the head. The answer is either yes or no. Then at least two improvisational statements confirming, and two denying whichever answer is chosen each night.*

Then each a suggestion on how you would act if you did *have frostbite in the head. There may be contradictions to the suggestions. From this, a composite characterization is arrived at for the role of the* BISHOP.

SERGEANT (*greatly angry*): All *RIGHT*! Then lis*TEN*! I want in-for-*MATION*! About this trai*TOR*. This war mon*GER*.

Who dipped his pen in poison,

And writ a century off to die.

PRIVATE: WE WANT TOM PAINE!

Repeat his name over and over. Search each other's faces for recognition. Search the theater. It mounts to hysteria. A witch hunt emerges. The disjointed calling becomes a concerted evocation of his name. From this emerges the street jargon song:

ALL: PAINE! PAINE!
DAMNED BE HIS NAME!
DAMNED BE HIS FAME!

23

AND LASTING HIS SHAME!
GOD DAMN PAINE! GOD DAMN PAINE!

In mathematical rotation each night, find the "ANI-MAL." Carry him on-stage on a pole or rifle. Stand him on a stool. Invest him with the physical characteristics of TOM PAINE. *Each add to his character of personal filth, his matted hair, his fingernails long as a rat's, his alcoholism, his twisted nose, his stunted body. Improvise the line and select bits of costuming and paint. In a frenzy of purging anger, create a scapegoat. Seed improvisational lines with these specifics:*

He came from Thetford.

From England.

He was Aquarius.

His father was a bastard.

His father made corsets.

He went to London. That pest hole.

He was 37 when he left.

He was exiled.

He was *not exiled*!

He went with a letter of recommendation from Benjamin Franklin.

And he crossed the ocean to America.

And he bade his friends good-by.

His friends were Goldsmith and the mystic Blake.

24

Lights dim. A ceremonial lifting of PAINE. *Place him center like an encircled, rutting animal.*

And he made the great crossing.

And he lived in a bear pit in New York.

ALL: AND HE MADE THE GREAT CROSSING!

All run off. Newly created TOM PAINE *center.* BISHOP *and* ALTAR BOY *with censer and incense, with font and evergreen branch. Chanting they go:*

BISHOP: May this house know no evil, no demons, no spirits, no creature of darkness, no manner of black and nefarious things, no blasphemers and damned adherents of Tom Paine. His heresy, his treason, his deceits, his lies and prevarications, and his murders and rebellions, his plots, his ploys, his intrigues. Ad infinitum.

Center, PAINE, *pound floor or resonating box. Offstage, group take notice. Begin to pound and make catcalls, noises, and distractions.*

If Satan has cause to point him across this threshold, may flames rise up from this consecrated ground, consume him, consume his feet, hair, and bones, consume his issue, and his issue's issue, and purify where he has trode. And may the Lord's angels who reign over these timbers and high vaults, the Lord's seraphim and cherubim who receive these prayers sent up, even as this incense is sent up to Him in the most high, may even they hear this sacred consecration and all know that herein dwells the Spirit of the most terrible and mighty Lord.

25

All pound with PAINE, *rhythmically.*

I'm not done yet!

ALTAR BOY: Hurry up your mouth.

BISHOP: I bless this house, this refuge for the homeless
of the war which he has caused and brought upon
us, may he burn in Hell. And I, the Lord's minion,
will see that pity shall not rebuff his swinishness.

ALTAR BOY: FASTER, they're impatient!

BISHOP: I will ferret out evil even as a hog roots out
truffles in this stinking barn living side by side with
those miserable bears . . . Christ, I lost my place . . .
His Holy war rages . . . which He in His perfectness
. . . His Highness the King . . . OH FUCK! His
Holy war rages, I read that!

ALTAR BOY: MOVE YOUR JAWS!

Throw the font at him.

BISHOP: In the name of the angels, the cherubim, and the
seraphim, *I CONSECRATE THIS HOUSE!*

Shimmy up rope to rafters. All rush in.

SONS OF BITCHES! YOU COULDN'T WAIT
TILL I WAS DONE?! COULD YOU?

Crowd these events, rapid, overlap on each other.

*A simple rocking form, like a children's playground
structure which volleys actors from floor to ceiling.
A sign: THE LONDON PACKET. Enormous sail
billows.*

26

ROGER, DODGER, BEULAH *center. Sign: GIN ROW.*

Bilge passengers limp, run, crawl to bilge. Pack into it knife-wedge tight. Moaning, shrieking, crying, panting, gasping, pound sides for air. Arms and legs grab out like wild animals. BISHOP *taunt them from above.*

All make sounds of seas, storms, groans, drumming. In this cacophony, all are sea-drunk, gin-drunk.

QUAKER (*in peruke*): This sea, this pit, this gutter of misery, this wallow called society . . . (*Pound gavel.*)

CAPTAIN: BLOW! LOOK AT 'ER BLOW!

MARIE: The Atlantic's waves are cold and bright,
      In the bilge below it's hot and tight,
      From London's sewers comes a man by name,
      Of fearful eye and burning roar,
      He brings with him the drums of war.

QUAKER *pound gavel.* DRUMMER *louder.* PAINE *laughs and all noises rise up. Heavy winds blow life into sail. The cacophony begins:*

CAPTAIN: Look at 'er blow! Lay out every inch of canvas you've got!

ROGER, *jump up and down laughing.* BEULAH *shrieking laughter.* DODGER *kneels under her skirt, bobbing voraciously. She kicks him out. All roar drunkenly.* BISHOP *above:*

MATE: If it'll hold wind, it's stretched taut already.

CAPTAIN: Look at 'er bounce! I'll bust the

BISHOP: SHUT UP, FILTHY BLEEDERS!

27

record for the cross-
ing!

*Deluge of garbage.
Roar anew.*

ROGER: You're drunk!

DODGER: Filthy drunk!

MATE: I'm feared we'll bust
the masts first.

ROGER: Cheap gin and
cheap sin. I'm for
Parliament and that's
my platform.

CAPTAIN: Let 'em bust!
She's damn near fly-
ing! It's a happy ship,
ain't she mate?!

DODGER: Them that ain't
drunk gets hanged.

ROGER: Then drawn and
quartered! Get all
London screaming
drunk! The whores
and babies and Par-
liament itself.
S C R E A M I N G
DRUNK!

MATE: Nine weeks of bash-
ing it out on the
water. Oh, a happier
ship never made the
crossing, Captain.

PAINE: MARIE! MORE BRANDY FOR THE DRUM-
MER! THE ARMY MARCH BEHIND HIM!
THEY NEED HIS BEAT! HURRY, THEIR
FEET BLEED IN THE SNOW!

All sing. Bilge cry refrain:

ALL: Look around London and what do you see?
Age to the poorhouse, youth to the gallows.
Because of-ffff . . .
GIN! GIN! GIN!
Enough to float the navy in.

28

GIN! GIN! GIN!
It's good for everything.
GIN! GIN! GIN!
Sores and pock holes, runny wham holes.
GIN! GIN! GIN!
WASH THE BABIES IN IT!
GIN! GIN! GIN!
THE GUTTERS RUN WITH IT!
GIN! GIN! GIN!

PAINE: IF THEY STOP NOW, THEIR FEET WILL FREEZE IN THE ROAD! THE ICE TEARS THE FLESH OFF THEIR FEET! MARIE, THE ROAD IS STIFF WITH BLEEDING FLESH!

CAPTAIN: MORE SAIL! LET 'EM BUST WIDE OPEN!

Main area. Read gently with calm measure:

Paine's body draped in Union Jack on deck. A cloth chute down side of ship.

OLD MAN: The bearer, Mr. Thomas Paine, is very well recommended to me as an ingenious worthy young man. He goes to Pennsylvania with a view of settling there. I request that you give him your best advice and countenance as he is quite a stranger there.

MATE: Captain, they're rottin' in the bilge down there. This un's the fifth to go on the crossin' and the bouncin' don't help none.

CAPTAIN: Have I ever let ye down, mate, in all our crossin's?

MATE: You been good to me, Captain. I'll

ROGER: SEND THE BAS-
TARD DOWN
HERE!

DODGER: SEND HIM
DOWN!

*Measured chorus of
pounding and insist-
ence.*

ALL: SEND HIM DOWN!
SEND HIM DOWN!

*Intermittent cries from
bilge throughout:*

Water!
Please!
God!
Gin!

BEULAH (*sings*):
If you're not blood
in England,
You are dirt.
For dirt in England,
Dirt breeds dirt.

swear on it, but it's
eatin' 'em up at a
smart rate. It's the
fever.

CAPTAIN: DON'T SAY
THAT WORD! Now,
Matey, you make out
a nice new passenger
list.

MATE: Showin' five less
than before, Captain?

CAPTAIN: Oh, yer a bright
lad!

MATE: And the finance
sheet'll show a little
adjustment too?

CAPTAIN: Oh, yer a bright
lad.

MATE: And maybe the
Captain'll see his way
clear to reward the
nice Matey?

CAPTAIN: Ain't you the
thoughtful one. Mind,
open your mouth in
town and you're shark
bait come the return
crossin'.

30

Slide Paine's body overboard into GIN ROW *group.*

NAKED CAME THEE OUT OF THY MOTHER'S WOMB, AND NAKED SHALL THEE RETURN THITHER! THE LORD GIVETH AND THE LORD TAKETH AWAY. BLESSED BE THE NAME OF THE LORD! WHERE'S THE GIN?!

Snatch him up, flag and all. Haul up by the feet. BISHOP *descend as counterweight.*

PAINE: BASTARDS! BASTARDS!

BEULAH: Gawd, caught him like a rat in a trap. Nabbed him proper. Lookit him. HEY! HEY!

ROGER: He's high as a kite.

BEULAH: Come on, give 'em a drink. He'll never get it up.

DODGER: Hanged man always gets it up.

ROGER: He's only sixteen.

31

BEULAH: I've seen it before. Come on, honey, I remember you.

Hussahs.

ALL: HE'S GOT A HARD-ON!

All sing:

GIN! GIN! GIN!
Enough to float the navy in.
GIN! GIN! GIN!
It's good for everything.

PAINE: BASTARDS! BASTARDS!

Cries, moans, pleas from the bilge.

THEY'RE BURNING THE BARNS! HIDING THE CATTLE! MY ARMY WILL STARVE! MARIE, THEY'RE SCORCHING THIS FROZEN HELL! BRANDY!

Bursts of laughter. Through the audience with electric bullhorn and lantern:

GIN SELLER: That's for cheap gin and cheap sin. Take your choice of slow death, horrible death, or blood-sloshing screaming death. That's a messy one. Tuppence gets you roaring drunk. Mothers swear by it. Kiddies shut their foul mouths for it. Try a can for courage. Push your old pa and his matrimonial sow off the roof. The legacy'll get you a barrel of my LIGHTNING FAST GIN!

PAINE: MARIE! THE ARMY RUNS AWAY! MARIE! THEY'VE DROPPED THEIR GUNS ON THE ROAD! MARIE! BRANDY! BRANDY!

32

GIN SELLER: It races up your spine. Snaps your nerves and tears up your guts! OW, IT'S LOVELY STUFF! LADIES! GENTS! BABIES! Screaming fits are free. Treat yourself to a holy vision of God and all his bleedin' saints in a BLINDING, FLASH-ING ELECTRICAL STORM! TRY MY LIGHT-NING GIN! Gawd, it's cheap enough.

Din in every quarter.

PAINE: DAMN THEM! DAMN THEM!

QUAKER: Hush thy sinful speech. If thy right arm offend thee, cut it off. If thy tongue speak evil, cut it out. A beating will teach thee to be a better Quaker.

PAINE: If there be God, God damn them. Curse Captain. Curse King. Curse God that brought forth thy kind and his greed. We are all animals with His fever.

QUAKER: I WILL BREAK THY HEAD! If thee die on the crossing, thee'll not be laid in holy ground to infect Christians.

PAINE: CURSE THY HOLY GROUND!

QUAKER: God grant thee be taken to the Devil himself. Praise be to Him Almighty.

PAINE: BASTARDS! BASTARDS ALL!

CAPTAIN: MORE SAIL! LET 'EM BUST WIDE OPEN!

ALL: WE'RE GOING TO AMERICA. THE PROM-ISED LAND!

Laughter, shrieks. Bilge floods out, moaning, crying, dazed by the light. With a long pole, pound for attention:

33

MAJOR DOMO: No sooner he landed than the sulphur of discontent blew in the air, and he sniffed it. And it excited him greatly. And he saw that it was good. The city was rife with rumors of war and treason. The taverns and the coffeehouses. And yes, the slave markets; the City of Brotherly Love wasn't brotherly. God had been whipped out of him long ago, yet he prayed to God these things:

PAINE (*say very quick without a breath or pause in whole speech*): Oh, God, what I have to do, I will do. I would do these things even if I did believe in Thee. Let us keep our peace between us a little longer, between Thee and me, you ancient Faker. I will get to Thee on a latter day. For now, I will set down on my papers other hatreds, between us and that other Royal faker who sits snorting German on his English throne, and I will drag him down. His little English corporals and his hired Hessian killers. Thou will see that I do these things.

Begin to carry him about.

And I will shake him off that perch and I WANT MYSELF TO TAKE UP THE KNIFE IN BOTH HANDS AND RIP OPEN HIS ROYAL SEAMS FROM HEAD TO BALLS! I want my words to go out like dogs biting at his heels. I'll tree him. I'LL TREE HIM! And while horns play and dogs yelp at his heels, I will take up the knife. And I will call this little book, this keg of sulphur and powder, I will tie its title like a fuse, *Common Sense*.

MAJOR DOMO: He wrote that book and, true to his promise, the dogs were unleashed and treason ran scream-

34

ing through the streets. His Reputation was born from the side of his rib.

Block it so that it is.

And now, it goes before him wherever he goes.

REPUTATION *in clean gray and white.*

Inside the City of Brotherly Love. Tom Paine and the Quaker.

QUAKER: This was once a good place. The City of Brotherly Love, The Peaceable Kingdom. Everyman was welcome here with open arms. Where a man could work and worship God in dignity. And the voice of the dove was heard in our land. And now . . .

PAINE: And now, Friend?

QUAKER: And now, thy black book, thine evil thou hast spawned on us . . .

PAINE: It is only Common Sense, Friend.

QUAKER: It is Satan's sense! Three HUNDRED THOUSAND copies or more, spread into every corner and it poisons minds wherever it goes. I have come to tell ye . . .

PAINE: To tell me that you don't approve of the war. Yet you don't approve either of the dead carted into the city under your nose.

QUAKER: Ye must stop writing thy filth! Ye must end this massacre ye have begun.

PAINE: It has begun. I cannot stop it, Friend. What are

we to do with the thousands of corpses fertilizing the fields around the city already? Close our eyes and bow our heads? What are we to do with the nasty details such as the 70,000 armed killers across the river, their bayonets pointed at our eyes this very minute?

QUAKER: Let the Congress settle that.

Group run on in panicked chaos, carrying bundles, bedding, chairs. CRIERS *ring hand bells, shout through electric bullhorn:*

CRIERS: The Congress urges everyone to stay in their homes. The roads are blocked. Stay at home! The roads are clogged. Stay at home for your own safety. CONGRESS HAS LEFT THE CITY! IT'S RUNNING FOR ITS LIFE! THE CITY IS RUNNING BEHIND IT!

PAINE: Now what is left of our army will have to slaughter itself to regain what the Congress threw away. There's the truth of it, good Friend.

QUAKER: The truth will come out by itself.

PAINE: The truth rarely comes out unless dragged by its hair. The seed crop of a whole generation dying to the last man to protect what? Those wise gentlemen who are supposed to guarantee order and happiness. They run with their tails between their legs, yelping, leaving the prize for the enemy.

Breaking glass. Books thrown from every quarter.

ALL: BURN THE DAMN BOOKS! BURN THEM! THROW THE TRASH IN THE STREET!

THEY'RE INVADING THE CITY FROM THE NORTH! THE ROADS ARE CUT OFF! THEY'RE SHELLING THE NORTH SECTION WITH ARTILLERY! THERE HE IS! GET HIM! THROW THE BASTARD IN THE FIRE! KILL HIM! KILL PAINE!

All attack PAINE, MARIE *fight them off.*

MARIE: STOP IT! STOP IT! He is laying out a blueprint for centuries to come. You want to kill him?!

PAINE: Marie, soon the angel will stalk over these hills and her cut will be clean and sure, and for so many, many, this life, this pageant, will be over.

MARIE: Go on, beat your crazy head. You're not God. You're just a man.

PAINE: That's sufficient.

REPUTATION: The war bewilders them.

PAINE: It was necessary.

Break. Be yourself. Light a cigarette if you want to. Actors, especially REPUTATION, *ask any questions you wish of the actor playing* PAINE, *concerning his true feelings and motivations. Suggestions:*

1. Why PAINE *brought about the revolution?*

2. Did he truly believe in the concept of independence enough to stir up a revolution?

3. Especially question why he hated the King on such an intense, personal level.

37

4. PAINE *actor, answer them yourself. Conclude with:*

ACTOR OF PAINE: He said nothing was so ridiculous as a king. He said, "Nature disapproved of kings or she wouldn't ridicule the folly so often by giving mankind an ass for a lion."

ACTOR OF REPUTATION: Do you think he would, if he could . . . like to be king himself?

ACTOR OF PAINE: That's ridiculous.

ACTOR OF MARIE: Did he hate the King . . . or did he envy him?

ACTOR OF PAINE: Neither. He believed in America. He christened the United States of America. They even picked his brains to write the Declaration of Independence!

ACTOR OF MARIE: We will see.

ACTOR OF PAINE: Tend to your bear pit,
                And leave this part to me.
                I'm Tom Paine.

Pause.

PAINE: I, Tom Paine. Land I have none. I have exiled myself from one country, without making a home of another. And sometimes, I cannot help asking myself, am I a revolutionary, or just a refugee.

MAJOR DOMO *with staff of office, announce:*

MAJOR DOMO: THE GENERAL. THE BISHOP. THE GOVERNOR.

Bow center in elegant costumes. Chamber music group play GIN song sweetly on your instruments. The three minuet.

Inside the Governor's palace.

GENERAL: Well now, just what are we to do with this girdle maker?

GOVERNOR: We'll do nothing. The whole thing will blow over.

GENERAL: On our heads. I say arrest him.

BISHOP (*obsequiously*): Gentlemen, the church has long experience in such matters as this. Over the centuries we have had to refine our sense of survival, and so have more experience in these matters. I say, let us wait and see.

GENERAL: Let the army arrest him and burn the damn books.

GOVERNOR: What will the people say?

GENERAL: The people! The people are like insane insects, forever rebuilding their destroyed houses. They'll survive.

BISHOP: We have to be clever. It's the book, you know. Books are dangerous. It's the book.

GOVERNOR: *Common Sense.*

GENERAL: Common Crap.

Dance ends.

BISHOP: Couldn't we . . . now let's see. Couldn't we somehow . . . tax the book?

BOTH: Tax?

GOVERNOR: They don't pay their other taxes. How can we collect on a book?

BISHOP: No . . . what if we tax *him*? Specifically, I mean, he sold thousands of these . . .

GENERAL: Little filth sheets.

BISHOP: We'll *invent* a tax. We'll tax his income on the book.

BOTH: What an absurd idea. A tax on income. Now this has possibilities, how did you think of that?

Someone hold a cymbal over his head.

BISHOP: Divine inspiration, my son.

MAJOR DOMO: Tom Paine's Reputation precedes him.

REPUTATION *kneel. They ride his back.*

The newspaper cartoons recorded the meeting.

Two follow them with cartoon balloon. They speak as written:

BISHOP: Church and Kings do bleſſ the land,
               Church and ſtate go hand in hand,

GENERAL: We ſuffer their bleſſings.

GOVERNOR: Upon our backs, the Junta rides,
               So ſoft they ſit upon our hides,

GENERAL: To feed and guide the poor and blind,
               They ſuck the taxes from our labor,

ALL: God bleſſ the King!

MAJOR DOMO: Tom Paine enters in a borrowed coat.

PAINE: Gentlemen, I am Thomas Paine, my respects.

GOVERNOR: Oh, we are pleased that you consider us gentlemen.

BISHOP: Yes.

GENERAL: Yes.

PAINE: You are the church. The state. And the military. Are you not?

GOVERNOR: We are.

BISHOP: *Yes*, we are.

ALL THREE: INDEED, we are!

GOVERNOR: How kind of you to acknowledge us, you . . .

(*Shrieking.*) YOU REBEL!

BISHOP: FATIN! BLAFPHEMER! HEREFY!

Grab him. Run him around.

GOVERNOR: Your book bloffomed treafon!

GENERAL: You, the army will fupreff and make you fuffer!

Throw PAINE down.

GOVERNOR: Gentlemen! Gentlemen, we are getting over-excited, and our diction gets sloppy when we get excited. NOW . . . no . . . EXCITEMENT! (*Calmly.*) No ex-cite-ment. Mr. Paine, we have read your book with great interest. (*Grunts.*)

PAINE: And so, my reputation speaks for me.

Both conversations melt into each other. PAINE, *drooling at the mouth as the* MAJOR DOMO *brings in a large brandy bottle.*

GOVERNOR: You realize the burdens of good government we have.

REPUTATION: That is precisely what I want to accomplish, good government. I have written the truth as I see it.

"The sun never shone on a cause of greater worth. 'Tis not the affair of a city, a country, a province, or a kingdom; but of a continent—of at least one-eighth part of the habitable globe. 'Tis not the concern of a day, a year, or an age; posterity are virtually involved in the contest, and will be more or less affected even to the end of time, by the proceedings now. Now is the seed-time of continental union and faith. The least fracture now will be like a name engraved with the point of a

Paine's hands shake, his mouth drools. He fumbles at the bottle.

PAINE: There they are, the fine gentlemen in their laces and lacquered pumps, their snuff-boxes of silver and their fine court manners, and the bottle on the table between us. Warm and red. See it shine. Just a sniff. That's all. A SNIFF! Ah, I can feel its perfume oozing through the cork. Ah . . . ah. (*Fumbles a great*

42

pin on the tender rind of a young oak; the wound would enlarge with the tree, and posterity read it in full grown characters. The Cause of America is in great measure the Cause of all Mankind."

drink.) No. No. Come away from it! Another? Just a small one. To steady my hand. I have to write all night, need a steady hand. Quick! Quick! Here they come. QUICK! ONE MORE! PLEASE!

GOVERNOR: You see I have the gout, Mr. Paine. The best doctors tell me to pickle my feet. It is so good for them.

Take off your boots as you speak. BISHOP *pour brandy on his feet.* PAINE *drool.*

BISHOP: A waste of good brandy.

GOVERNOR: In the interests of good government.

GENERAL: A governor in pain is apt to be a cross governor.

GOVERNOR: And it soothes the feet so. A waste of good brandy? Is that what you are thinking, Mr. Paine?

BISHOP: It shouldn't go to waste, should it, Mr. Paine?

GENERAL: Oh, don't let it go to waste.

GOVERNOR: Waste is wasteful. Go on.

GENERAL: Don't waste it. Go on, lick it up.

PAINE *slobber over his feet.*

BISHOP: Lick it all. Between the toes.

43

GENERAL: Lick it up, best brandy of Jamaica.

BISHOP: We know you appreciate good brandy.

PAINE (*to* REPUTATION): HYPOCRITE! Get out if you can't stand to watch!

GENERAL: We've heard you can lap up your weight in brandy.

GOVERNOR: Now dry my foot.

BISHOP: With your hair.

GOVERNOR: There sits the American Revolution.

Change costumes laughing and grunting like animals.

MARIE: There sits Paine. A tramp. Paine a beggar. There he sits, warming his guts now for a fight. Revolution breeds like a boil in his mind to tear down whole cities, and all the continents of the fat round world will bleed from his surgery. It folds like a fist in his brain.

MALE: And sure as he promised, the armies formed sides, and death, the mad woman, ran screaming over the land.

The RITE OF EXORCISM *begins to form. Recite lines in rotational form.*

PAINE, *breathlessly jerk the word out between gasps of air:*

PAINE: The two men . . . shook hands. One had gloves. One had . . . socks over his hands. Brown wool. The two men stood. No. One was already mounted

44

to horse. Only one man stood. The other began to curl a smile. He shook hands instead. His mouth would not smile. He was ashamed. His teeth were wood. He did not smile. OH, CHRIST, GIVE ME A DRINK!

ALL: *Go on!*

MALE: The famous woman in the red cloak enters.

WOMAN: God has sent me with a message for you.

PAINE: 'Tis a lie! He would not send his messages by such an ugly woman.

WOMAN: Recant! For your judgment is near.

ALL: *THE FIT COMES ON YOU!*

WOMAN: Fast as fire.

ALL: THE FIT COMES ON YOU!

She hovers over him.

Sucking the air from his fire.

ALL: *RECANT! FOR GOD!*

They'll curse you.

They'll teach their children filth in verse for you.

PAINE: 'Tis a lie! They wished Godspeed. They departed. Slow retreat into November. The nights grow longer. THE COLD TURNED THESE FINGERS BLUE! Retreat drags from campfire to campfire . . . to disintegration. Deserters take rags from their feet. Pad horses' hooves. Steal away on snow. He wanted to smile, but he was ashamed of his

45

ALL: *IN VERSE SO THEY WON'T FORGET!*

They'll ape your face and your long nails.

That curl around your toes.

You'll have to fight for every inch of history you take up.

The British voyeurs watched and giggled.

Like towel girls in a whorehouse.

WOMAN: RECANT!

ALL: *THE RITE OF EXORCISM!*

The smell of barracks.

A woman is raped.

A boy is raped.

An army starves in the snow.

teeth. They geed the horses. One went on his journey to the South.

GODSPEED! 'TIS A LIE!

There stood the German Hessians like a giant phallus, loaded and pointed at the buttocks of Trenton. There we, gyved up and bound, trembling and waiting, cooking our belts for hunger's sake.

'TIS A LIE!

We, stripped naked and bare, braced for the attack like runners in a heat, head down, hands down, buttocks up, trembling and waiting for the shot. The German battering ram pounded at us.

(Husky, very upper registers of your voice, drawing for air, very quickly:)

46

ALL: **A WHOLE ARMY!**
A young boy is eaten in secret.

The cannibals weep as they eat.

ALL: They pick his brains to mold . . . *The United States of America.*

They hunt him down with dogs.

ALL: *RECANT! RECANT!*

(*Surround the* SERGEANT.)

The war poor, mouths dumb with hunger.

Too swollen to speak.

ALL: *Pointed to their mouths like nesting birds.*

Like crows.

ALL: *Like birds!*

Stole the belts to suck the flavor.

I ran starving through those icy lanes under the arches of nut trees. Picked clean. I saw a lone cabbage, blue with frost. Still there. I cracked it open like a stone and ground it in my teeth. The whole head of it. I crept into that house by the nut trees. Picked clean. The windows cataracted with frost. I crept in past the sleepers in their beds, and into an empty room and gnawed the stalk of cabbage, blue with frost. And outside the bells rang, and the bleeding feet shuffled past on the rock hard earth.

(*Say inhaling a single breath of air. Say quickly and stacatto. Voice register higher and higher:*)

And high. High. Hi. Hi . . . hi above. Miles

47

CANNIBAL THINGS HAP-PENED!

The fresh-killed soldiers . . .

(*Two soldiers carried on poles, semi-naked. Bite into them.*)

. . . flung like slaughtered sheep in the fields.

Tempting the appetite.

Tender and young.

ALL: *TEMPTING THE APPETITE!*

Watering juices in the mouth.

up. We below as black ants. Creep. In the snow. Devour. Eat. Chew. Crack. Marrow. Body and blood. Of God. *Sacred. Christmas. Night.* The Star! Of. Beth. Up. Up. High. In. Excelsis. Deo. DON'T STAND THERE! HELP ME!

Dialogues end together. Two women GREEDIES *wipe the feast from your mouths. Sing and dance to accompaniment. Intermittent belches of satisfied gluttony from group, as you play your instruments sweetly.*

DUET OF THE GREEDIES: Tom Paine came from afar, afar,
His nose is like a blazing star.
He stirred the world around and round.

48

And turned the heavens upside down.

MAJOR DOMO *pound staff*.

MAJOR DOMO: Filthy and drunk, he wrote the great
Crisis paper.

REPUTATION: My hands sweat. How to yea-say this
slaughter. All the notes. All the papers.

PAINE: Get it the way it should say.

REPUTATION: How to yea-say these things to history.

PAINE: NOT BRAY!

REPUTATION: Pray?

PAINE: CRAP THAT CRUTCH!

> REPUTATION, *speak calmly*. PAINE, *mime your
> mouth to the words and speak together at appro-
> priate places*.

REPUTATION: The treasure of the world cannot induce
me to support an offensive war, for I think it murder.
But if a thief breaks into my house, burns and
destroys my property, and kills those that are in it,
and to *"bind me in all cases whatsoever"* to his abso-
lute Kingly will, am I to suffer from it? Let them
call me rebel and welcome! I feel no concern from
it. But I should suffer the misery of the devil, were
I to make a whore of my soul by swearing alle-
giance to one whose character is that of a sottish,
stupid, stubborn, worthless, brutish man. I call not
upon a few, but upon all; not of this state or that
state, but of every state. Let it be told to the future

world, that in the depth of winter when nothing but hope could survive, that the country alarmed at one common danger came forth to meet and to repulse it.

Drum roll.

MAJOR DOMO: And it was repeated down the line. Down the line. "Let it be told. In the depth of winter."

Send the phrases down the line.

MARIE: The rebels won the battle!

MAJOR DOMO: But off Sandy Hook 200 cannon had erections. And on the ships stood a thousand soldiers. And they were all erect. The Lord Admiral was in command of all these erections. And he said:

BLACK DICK (*very nasal in Admiral's hat*): *This* is unnatural.

MAJOR DOMO: This many cannon. This many soldiers.

BLACK DICK: In *this* condition.

MAJOR DOMO: He issued a proclamation.

Drum roll.

DRUMMER: His Lordship, Admiral Richard Howe.

BLACK DICK: ALL RIGHT! Enough of this. Now lay down your arms. Good heavens, down. And, umm, now, you see. These soldiers and . . . ummm, SOME of these, ummmm, sailors. Mine. Umm, yes, they are mine. WE WANT TO MAKE SUE-UR-AH, THAT UMM, THIS SORT OF THING does not, umm, RE-occurah. Do you he-ah? And umm, that our-ah Lord. That is, umm George. The Thahrd I believe?

MARIE: Yes, the Thahrd.

BLACK DICK: Is paid prop-ah, ah . . . ah . . . ALLE-GIANCE. Yes. You see, he, umm, paid for all this. SO! That. Is, umm, my proclamation.

Applaud him.

MAJOR DOMO: In the streets, in Five Points, they loved it.

DRUMMER: Signed, Lord Admiral Richard Howe.

BEULAH: That's not his name.

BLACK DICK: All right, big mouth.

BEULAH: His name's Black Dick. It really was.

Throw your hat at her. Square dance. All sing:

ALL: (*Refrain.*)
Who can take you serious
When your name's Black Dick.

When brains were passed around the floor,
Black Dick stood behind the door. (*Refrain.*)

They put their money on his nose,
Black Dick stood and there he froze. (*Refrain.*)

They bet that he would rise and shine,
Black Dick's horse was left behind. (*Refrain.*)

Nobility is bound to rise,
Why should it come as a surprise.

Crossover 1:

QUARTERMASTER: Look Private! You ain't gettin' no boots from my storeroom without you got the proper chit. If we had any boots. Which we ain't.

PRIVATE: I got one good one.

QUARTERMASTER: Where did you get it?

PRIVATE: From a dead Hessian. All I need is one to match it up.

QUARTERMASTER: Sorry.

PRIVATE: So I got to shoot another Hessian?

QUARTERMASTER: Yeeep.

PRIVATE: With what? I'll have to kick him to death with my one good boot.

QUARTERMASTER: Yeeep.

Crossover 2: Two old DEAF WOMEN *with ear trumpets.*

1ST DEAF WOMAN: The lists show three shiploads of boots and ammunition came into port.

2ND DEAF WOMAN: What?

1ST DEAF WOMAN: It all disappeared.

2ND DEAF WOMAN: What?

1ST DEAF WOMAN: The lists are stamped Hortalez and Company.

2ND DEAF WOMAN: What?

1ST DEAF WOMAN: IT'S ALL DISAPPEARED!

2ND DEAF WOMAN: You don't have to shout.

MAJOR DOMO *pound staff for attention.*

MAJOR DOMO: THE SILAS DEANE AFFAIR! This is the last scene in the first act. We trust it will please you. The Court of St. James and the Palace of Versailles.

Black and red patent-leather groundcloth unrolled. It is a chessboard.

We call this chess game the Steinitz Gambit, in honor of that genius who had a fondness for the maxim, "The King is a fighting piece." You will play:

Pound staff at presentations. Each enters in red or black velvet collars and all in large mask-peruke headpieces.

Monsieur Caron de Beaumarchais. (Bow.) You wrote the Marriage of Figaro but you were born to a low life and so spend the rest of your time pimping your talents at court. Red Rook. Position 1.

Mr. Silas Deane. (Bow.) A merchant to act as American agent in Paris. You are worse than a dog tick. You bloat yourself on war profits as your kind has always done. Color the blood in your veins, green for greed. (*Like a sentence of guilt:*) Black Knight. Position 2.

Mr. Arthur Lee. (Bow.) You are really a damn fool, but the author suspects you are incapable of hatching large intrigues in your small brain. Red Pawn. Position 3.

53

Enter on roller skates. Face hooded. No bow for you.

You, *A British Spy.* Oh, go on! Black Pawn. Position 4.

Ministre de France in America, Phillippe Gerard. (*Bow.*) You are the twitching, itching, limping, blinking skilled diplomat always in these events. Red Knight. Position 5.

Gouverneur Morris. (*Bow. Red side hiss him.*) You are the knife an old idea fights with but nobody sees the hand on it. It's an old trick, and you're a master of it. Black Rook. Position 6.

The Prime Minister of France, Count de Vergennes. (*Bow.*) Good evening, your Excellency. We are pleased you could come. Please, would you be so kind. Red Knight. Position 7.

Now let's see. (*Pause.*) Oh. *The American Committee of Secret Correspondence.* (*Bow. Hooded.*) Black Rook. Position 8.

Mr. John Jay, President of Congress. (*Bow.*) You are a snob and I suspect a bigot. Black Pawn. Position 9.

Mister Thomas Paine. Since this scene vitally concerns you, I suggest you stand center. On the Red side. Position 10.

And now, gentlemen (*Black side to attention*), His Majesty, George III, *The King of England.*

Giant wig, cloak, pumps, and crown. Black side bow low. Red side hiss and catcall.

Gentlemen, His Majesty, Louis XVI, *The King of France.*

Giant wig, cloak, pumps, and crown. Red side bow low. Black side hiss and catcall.

As you see, there are no recognizable land masses, but on either side, ideas as firm as continents. And in between a sea of differences. And on either shore, mankind plays at being hateful spiders. Instead of spinning silk.

Each side hiss and insult the other side loudly.

LOUIS XVI: SILENCE! SILENCE!

GEORGE III: SCHWEIG! SCHWEIGEN!

MAJOR DOMO *pound your staff. Slowly, taunting:*

LOUIS XVI: 'E ees ze King of England, et 'e cannot even speek eenglish as goud as . . . me do.

GEORGE III: SCHWEINEHUND! DAS IST ZUM KNOCHEN KOTZEN!

MAJOR DOMO *do pound your staff for silence.*

LOUIS XVI (*to* BEAUMARCHAIS): What did 'e say?

BEAUMARCHAIS: Pardon, mon roi. Il a dit . . . conch.

LOUIS XVI: Conch? CONCH! CONCH LUI-MÊME!

GEORGE III: FRANZÖSISCHES SCHWEIN!

MAJOR DOMO: Count de Vergennes, advance to position, Red King 2.

Move in the manner of the chess piece you are.

55

COUNT: Sire, last night I had a dream. A divine inspiration worthy of your attention.

LOUIS XVI: Invent for me a knife big enough to cut loose that miserable little English island tied to the coast of *our France* and let it float to . . . to Terre de Fuego.

COUNT: Sire, I cannot do that. Besides, your brother-in-law owns Terre de Fuego.

LOUIS XVI: Bien, then it would be his problème.

COUNT: We can do better than that. We can keep this little war in America boiling by giving the rebels monies to purchase ammunition, gunpowder, boots and thereby divert enough of the English armies to fight the rebels, so they will not be a threat to your Majesty. We give this to the rebels under the fictitious name of Hortalez and Company, so the British spies will never know the money comes from us. And who knows, the rebels might even win. *And who knows,* he (*pointing to* GEORGE III) might even lose his American Colonies. What do you think that would do to his gout?

LOUIS XVI: How much will your "divine inspiration" cost us?

COUNT: About two million livres.

LOUIS XVI: DEUX MILLION! You and your divine inspiration are crazy!

COUNT: But you see, Sire, we would give the rebels all the army's outdated ammunition which we would have to melt anyway. They will do the fighting for us. And you can appreciate what the loss of America would mean to the King.

LOUIS XVI: Divine inspiration!

COUNT: I am pleased you like my plan.

LOUIS XVI: Whose plan?

COUNT: Your plan, Sire. We will use Beaumarchais.

LOUIS XVI: That clockmaker. I can't stand him.

COUNT: Exactly, Sire. If anything goes wrong, he will be the ah . . . ah . . .

BOTH: . . . the ah . . . (*laugh*) the scapegoat.

LOUIS XVI: I love it. Call him in.

MAJOR DOMO: Beaumarchais to position Red King 2.

BEAUMARCHAIS (*stuttering*): I-I-I will es-establish a fictitious company. I-I-I will call it Hortalez and Company.

MAJOR DOMO: Beaumarchais to Red Pawn 3.

BEAUMARCHAIS: Mr. Arthur Lee, American Agent in London, Hortalez and Company will give you two million livres in ammunition. Don't tell anyone it is a gift from Louis Seize, because if the English knew this, they would bomb us off the face of the earth.

MAJOR DOMO: Arthur Lee to the American Committee of Secret Correspondence. Position 2. British Spy follow him.

Red side hiss them.

ARTHUR LEE (*W. C. Fields delivery*): Wonderful news. France will give us supplies free of charge.

MAJOR DOMO: Arthur Lee *check*. (*Off the board.*) Silas Deane to Secret Committee. Position 2. Spy free to rove about.

COMMITTEE (*weasel nasal*): Mister Deane, you will go to Paris. You will contact Hortalez and Company and get the goods.

DEANE (*drawl*): What about mah five per cent commission? I always get mah five per cent commission.

COMMITTEE: Mister Deane, you are doing this for your country. You understand that, don't you Mister Deane?

DEANE: Fine. Then I get mah five per cent commission from the country. I always get mah five per cent commission.

COMMITTEE: Mister Deane, it is so easy to love you. Heh, heh, heh. Good-by, Mister Deane.

MAJOR DOMO: Silas Deane to Count de Vergennes. At this point the wires get crossed. Watch carefully.

COUNT: You will go to Beaumarchais and say I sent you. These vital supplies are a *gift* from France. You understand that, Mister Deane?

DEANE: I always get mah five per cent commission.

MAJOR DOMO: Count de Vergennes *check*. (*Off the board.*) Deane to Beaumarchais.

BEAUMARCHAIS: Ah, mais non, Monsieur. Are you crazy? A gift?

DEANE: Ah thought Mistah Lee was crazy. If this was a gift, how was ah getting mah five per cent commission? I always get mah five per cent commission.

BEAUMARCHAIS: Of course, if it were a gift, I would not get my ten per cent commission. Already we sent three ships of supplies. The British she confiscated two, but you can be sure I will have to charge your Congress for all three.

DEANE: Mah commission is five per cent. I always get mah five per cent commission, Mistah Beau-marchais.

MAJOR DOMO: Deane to Secret Committee.

COMMITTEE: Mister Deane, you realize if this affair comes to the attention of Congress . . . well, Mister Deane, we are the SECRET Committee. We shall keep our little secret. No one must hear of this two million livres. Our little secret.

DEANE: Mistah Committee, our little two million secret is now a great big four million secret. And here's mah bill.

SPY *to* GEORGE III.

COMMITTEE: Oh . . . no . . . Mister Deane . . .

MAJOR DOMO: Secret Committee *check*. (*Off the board.*)

DEANE: And I'm going to take this heah matter to the people.

MAJOR DOMO: Silas Deane makes a public address to Congress.

DEANE: "The Address of Silas Deane to the Free and Virtuous Citizens of Amuuuurrrrica!"

Great noises from everyone.

LOUIS XVI: I know nothing about this! *Beaumarchais! Idiot!*

BEAUMARCHAIS: Oui, m-m-mon roi.

LOUIS XVI *finger across throat: "Kkkkkrrrrhhhh!"*

MAJOR DOMO: Beaumarchais, *check.* (*Off the board.*) British Spy, *check.* (*Off the board.*)

LOUIS XVI: SILENCE! SILENCE! And you can stop performing his plays. He does not *exist* anymore!

GEORGE III: SCHWEIG! SCHWEIGEN!

LOUIS XVI: Why don't you speek Eenglish, if you can?!

GEORGE III: FRANSÖSISCHES SCHWEIN! We will see who can spricht besser English! Your own guillotine? Kkkkkrrrrhhh! UND we will see who can spricht . . . ohne A HEAD!

LOUIS XVI: Qu-qu-qu'est-ce qu'il a dit?

GERARD: Oh, rien, mon roi.

MAJOR DOMO: Paine to John Jay, President of Congress.

Purse mouth at each period.

J. JAY: Mister Paine. I won't banter words. Everyone knows I'm no admirer of yours. But since you are Secretary of the Committee of Foreign Affairs. You should be in a position to unravel. This conundrum.

60

PAINE: Mr. Jay, HOW IN THE NAME OF HEAV-
EN . . .

J. JAY: Hear! Hear!

MORRIS: Mr. Paine, do guard your language.

PAINE: Mr. Morris, if the soldiers do not have guns, you
will have to guard your private . . .

J. JAY: Mr. Paine, if you have something to say, say it
with a civil tongue.

MORRIS: This Congress is composed of gentlemen.

MARIE: Tread carefully.

REPUTATION: You walk on egg shells.

PAINE: I'll walk on their heads! Mr. Jay, since I am not
a gentleman . . .

MORRIS: Obviously.

PAINE: . . . you will have to guide me in those delicate
matters. All that stands between this city and the
40,000 bayonets poised at our throats is a small
band of freezing farmers who have to repeat out
loud to themselves that they are soldiers when
they know they are not. Would this august body of
gentlemen tell me why the warehouses of the city
are breaking with uniforms and boots and powder,
guarded by private police when the soldiers are
freezing to death. Daily! When those very supplies
were . . .

DEANE: LIES! THE FILTHY DRUNKEN BEGGAR
LIES!

PAINE: . . . were given to the army as a gift!

J. JAY: Note that down.

GERARD: The rat falls into the trap.

MORRIS: Let him hang himself.

PAINE: A GIFT! FREE AND CLEAR!

J. JAY: Remember your oath of silence.

PAINE: Silence is not in my nature. This profiteer claims he served the public. He served his pockets.

DEANE: I have been of grrrrreat service to the cause.

PAINE: God save us from what *you* have done. What any of you have done.

J. JAY: Does this accusation include the Congress, Mr. Paine?

Pause.

MORRIS: Well, Mr. Paine? The question "tumbles" through the air.

PAINE: When the Congress should have stood their ground, did they?

J. JAY: The Congress could not be allowed to fall into enemy hands, Mister Paine.

PAINE: The Congress should have stayed in the city.

J. JAY: Note that down.

MORRIS: The trap is sprung.

DEANE: I did mah duty, and I followed orders.

PAINE: You?! You lived very well indeed while the soldiers half-starved and half-naked waited for your

62

supplies. And never did men grow so old in so short a time. They crowded the business of an age into a few short months while you haggled prices on those supplies which were a *gift* from Louis Capet even before you arrived in France!

MAJOR DOMO: Secret revealed.

GEORGE III: SO!

LOUIS XVI: Gerard, you idiot, maneuver!

GERARD: Those supplies were no gift. They were *bought* from the King's magazines and arsenals in Paris. His Majesty did not *give* anything away.

LOUIS XVI: Bravo, Gerard!

GERARD: And I protest these indiscreet assertions. And I wish you to take measures suitable for divulging secrets.

REPUTATION: Now you've done it.

Huddle and confer.

J. JAY: Mr. Paine, the Foreign Committee, I regret to say, has no further need for your services.

MORRIS: Paine. Check. And checkmate.

PAINE: I don't give a damn about the Foreign Committee. What about the supplies? The King still has his sleeve full of tricks.

J. JAY: Don't concern yourself with the King. He is our affair now.

MORRIS: Again, you go into the streets. Where you belong.

DEANE: Troublemaker.

MORRIS: You can be the king of the streets.

J. JAY: You will leave. Go away!

MORRIS: Leave!

ALL: Leave!

PAINE: Why do I do it! Jackasses dressed up in gold braid, timid mice scurrying underfoot! Eating me a piece at a time.

REPUTATION: Your work is done.

PAINE: That's what you think! I'm not done yet with the "majestic" German. Give me a drink!

Each side menacingly to other side:

BLACKS: No!

REDS: GIVE HIM A DRINK!

MAJOR DOMO: The war in America will be over soon. He lit a fire, and now Europe is a seething caldron set to boil over and scald everything in its path. England and France are about to *crack open the face of Europe.* And nothing will ever be the same again.

KINGS *stand on shoulders and circle for battle.*

LOUIS XVI: Conch . . . conch . . . CONCH ALLEMAND!

GEORGE III: Klotz . . . klotz . . . FRANSÖSISCHER KLOTZ!

THE BATTLE. *Both sides in melée of insults, trying to drag* KINGS *down, defending-assaulting.* KINGS *fall.*

64

Each side tears crowns and regalia from other side's KING. KINGS *chased off board.*

MAJOR DOMO: Exit the pomp of power!

PAINE: The revolution will be won. *Oh, it will be won!* And then . . .

REPUTATION: And then?

PAINE: Then I'll carry it to his doorstep.

ALL: To England!

REPUTATION: You're meat for his jaws.

PAINE: I'll snatch the meat from his jaws. Give me a drink!

ALL: GIVE HIM A DRINK!

Revert to characters you were in the beginning of the act. Rotational lines:

You've got to be a king to fight it out with a king.

Step center and stop action.

SERGEANT: All right . . . ALL RIGHT! I WANT TO KNOW SOMETHING ABOUT TOM PAINE! THIS TRAITOR!

MARIE: Did this help you any, Sergeant?

Start to dress PAINE *in both kings' regalia.*

SERGEANT: Help?! I DIDN'T UNDERSTAND A DAMN WORD OF IT!

MARIE: The moment's passed, you'll understand it later. Give him this.

SERGEANT: What are you doing now?

MARIE: Give him this!

Everyone now assist in the investiture.

PAINE:　　　　GIVE ME A DRINK! Stop that. STOP IT!

Get dressed. You'll love it.

It's velvet.

And ermine.

REPUTATION: What are you doing to him?! Stop this!

He's getting good and drunk.

It's got all this gold stuff.

See it shine?

It's real . . . almost.

Just an arm.

Come on.

PAINE:　　　　GIMME 'NOTHER DRINK!

The other arm.

BISHOP:　　　The investiture of the King.

The livery of royalty.

He is drunk. Mockingly, continue to clothe him.

And the robes.

Red ones.

RED!

So red they're black.

PAINE:　　　　Mine must be as red as his.
They're even redder than his.

66

REPUTATION: STOP, YOU WITLESS FOOL! THEY'RE PUTTING WORDS IN YOUR MOUTH!

And . . . and . . . the fingernails.

PAINE: Gilt! Gilt, please, Marie.

They're gilded thrice over.

More gilded than even his.

And longer than even his.

And . . . and . . . the gloves of state.

That touch without being touched.

Silver gloves.

Stiff silk.

Stiffer than even his.

GIVE-ME-A-DRINK! All you ministers, get it up. ARE YOU LISTENING? Like a hanging man. I shall surely see him hang! You . . . YOU! You're not trying! Harder! A silver bell is supposed to ring when it occurs. You're only halfway there. MINISTERS I CANNOT HEAR YOUR SILVER BELLS!

A forceful carillon of bells. Maybe hanging pipes.

I am ready to be horsed

He is lifted up.

And the sceptre.

ALL: THE SCEPTRE!

PAINE: It must be gold.

67

Golder than even his.

REPUTATION: STOP THIS!

PAINE: WHERE'S MY ORB?! AND MY
BRANDY?!

Your orb.

More continents than even his.

AH! AH! AH! And . . . and . . . the dia
. . . NOT DIADEM, IDIOTS! THE BAS-
TARD NEVER WEARS A DIADEM!

REPUTATION: STOP IT, YOU FOOL! (*Try to stop them.*)

BISHOP: He wears . . . (*whisper*) the crown.

PAINE: Marie, he wears the crown.

With jewels.

CRUST THEM ON ME! I am ready
for . . . for . . . the . . . ah . . . ah . . .
crowwwwwwnnnn.

BISHOP: The investiture is complete.

PAINE: I will go to his doorstep, and I will bring my
revolution and the war and the massacre to him.
Give me seven years, just seven, and I will write
a Common Sense for every nation in Europe. And
I will go to France, and I will decree my imprison-
ment in the dungeons of Luxembourg, and the
fateful cross of chalk on my door, and possibly my
own decapitation on the guillotine. Ohhhh, a king's
a lovely thing.

SERGEANT: I DON'T UNDERSTAND A DAMN
WORD OF THIS!

MARIE: Well, Sergeant, we're tired now. We'll try again later. He says he'll go to England, but before he goes, let's take a break to consider if he should.

SERGEANT: All right, but when you tell it this time, I don't want no nonsense. I want you to talk straight! Do you hear?!

ALL (*mocking*): Oh, we will, Sergeant.

Start to straggle off singing "Tom Paine came from afar, afar." It grows and grows, louder and louder with drums, gongs, and noises.

SERGEANT: Allllll right. All right! ALL RIGHT! ALL RIGHT! ! !

PRIVATE *try to drum them to silence. Add to the cacophony.*

Only PAINE *and* REPUTATION *left on stage. He stands stunned in disarray of regalia.*

REPUTATION: "Turned the world upside down," head-hunting kings. And there you are.

REPUTATION *exit, disgusted. Pause.* MARIE *enter. Address audience.*

MARIE: All right, you can go out for a smoke now, it's intermission.

Leave PAINE *on stage in full light throughout intermission.*

CURTAIN

SCENES IN PART TWO:

PART TWO

Straggle on. Clear light. Rotational:

Do you have the bag. Of turtles.

TURTLES?!

More animals in this show.

Bears. Turtles. What's next?

If there were three acts, we'd have elephants.

They didn't expect to see a bear anyway. Did you?

It's not a zoo, you know. It's just a stage.

And it's full of splinters.

And the dressing rooms are *tacky.*

Come backstage after the show, you'll see.

Oohh, Marie has had her pee.

And she's feeling ballsy.

Again.

MARIE: All right, ready for another crack at it, Sergeant?

SERGEANT: Just a minute. *Just a minute.*

> *Get gun. Put on hat.*

> Now, where were we?

MARIE: You want Tom Paine. You've come to the bear pit where he lives, in Lower Manhattan.

You've got an arrest warrant.

As long as your arm.

Drum roll.

SERGEANT: Tom Paine wanted for sedition and treason whose whereabouts are known to be in this vicinity of Five Points. By order of General Burgoyne, Commander of this here district.

BISHOP: We went back to England.

MARIE: Wake him up.

Wake PAINE.

PAINE: Let me alone.

MARIE: Get in the boat. We're going to England.

PAINE: Oh, let me sleep.

BISHOP: It was dark when he sailed. I'm afraid of the dark.

The American Revolution is won.

MARIE: He swore he'd bring it to England.

And to France.

SERGEANT: All right, let's begin. Take out the house lights!!

BISHOP: I . . . I'm afraid in the dark.

SERGEANT: Take down the dimmers, across the light board!!

72

BISHOP: I . . . I'm afraid in the dark!

MARIE: Get the turtles. You'll be all right.

MAJOR DOMO: Part Two. Blake receives Paine at the coast amid the turtle stars.

Ship rock quietly to and fro with cloaked figures. Use image of Blake's "Pity." PAINE *in black mask with burning diamond eyes and black cloak.*

CHILDREN, *fore-center, take turtles from bag. Turtles have small birthday-size candles on their backs, lit. In the dark as they crawl about,* WINDS *and* WAVES *whisper-chant.*

SENTRIES *stretch out arms and hold hands.*

ALL: THE NIGHT FIXES THE EARTH BALL!

PAINE: The night fixes the earth ball, and I long to lever it round once more.

BISHOP (*sobbing*): Please, it's dark, dark. Please . . . hold me.

CHILDREN (*sing*): Here lies the body of Jim Crow,
Who was high, but now is low.
Ye brother Crows, take warning all,
For as ye rise, so must ye fall.

WINDS AND WAVES: Oh and oh, and oh and oh, the winds sighed song for the sightless horses of the waves. The penny pot of ink sways and sways. And oh and oh, the ship a-pitch in the night, slipped in the ocean shining bright. Pad the waves, pad their hooves. His cargo is velvet black. The penny pot of ink is very black. And oh and oh, through the

73

mists and through the waves, and on the sightless horses, two eyes burned and yearned and burned the light of madmen, to hook the coast of England in their light.

TWO SENTRIES: Two sentries on the coast of England. Our arms stretched out to tell the sea, this for you and this for us, and all of ours. Sea, this is where you leave. This patch, this rock is ours and beyond in those deeps lies yours. This coast, our arms stretched out, say to everyone, *This is England.*

WINDS AND WAVES: Wave-ferried ship in the night, outwit the stars. *To England.* And the penny pot of ink sways and sways. The bite and crack of its words still lie scrambled, jumbled-tumbled-viscous-black in the penny pot. Waiting for the dip. Of the pen. Of the man. Called Paine. (*Inhale "Ah":*) Ah, but the penny pot of ink sways and sways.

TWO SENTRIES: Sea, wherever you're from, whatever you've seen, whatever you bring in your corked and salty whispers, say to brine and man alike, *This is England.*

WINDS AND WAVES: Sways and sways.

TWO SENTRIES: Ride a cocked horse to Banbury Cross to London Tower and to St. James Court. Tell the King to flail the waters, to punish the waves for their treason.

PAINE: This is an age of treason.

WINDS AND WAVES: The mystic Blake knows secret things.

BLAKE *enter in cloak.*

74

BLAKE: Solemn heave the Atlantic waves between the gloomy nations.

WINDS AND WAVES: Sways and sways.

BLAKE: A cowl of flesh grow o'er his head and scales on his back and ribs. "Things" in rustling scales rush into reptile coverts!

Inhale "whale" and "away":

Where wolves and tygers howl for prey,
I see a whale drinking my soul away.

All run off except SENTRIES. KING GEORGE III *enter hurriedly and flail angrily.*

SENTRIES: The sea trembles like a murderer and swells *to wash the shores of England clean.*

All run before the waves. Immediately:

MAJOR DOMO: It is now summer. The heavens continue to do their job beautifully. Rain falls, sun shines, blessings for the bounty of man continue, and nature's philanthropy is lobbied for by witch doctors and farmers around the world. Mankind accepts it all, and gripes for more. The Church in France gluts itself on over one-half of the entire land, belches its gut clear and demands in a loud voice not to be taxed.

ALL: YOU KNOW WHO PAYS THE TAXES!

MAJOR DOMO: Ancient feudal leftovers, divine rights of kings, hungry courts, a gluttonous church. France has it all. And nobody pays a sou in taxes.

ALL: YOU KNOW WHO PAYS!

75

MAJOR DOMO: Eat and eat and eat some more is a duty to the state.

ALL: YOU KNOW WHO EATS!

MAJOR DOMO: Louis in France. George in England. One a locksmith. One a farmer. Neither went half a mile without a swarm of toadies, overdressed and over-perfumed. All eating. Every step of the way.

ALL: AND THE PEOPLE WORK OVERTIME!

MAJOR DOMO: So they could wake up and *eat* some more. Things are ripe for Paine and his fresh, hybrid, crazy way of looking at things.

ALL: BLOW SOME AIR INTO THIS LILLIPUT OF CRAP, PRETENSE, AND BULLSHIT!

MAJOR DOMO: Oh, happy is the land ruled by a king.

Projecting frontal platforms. Union Jack over one. Fleur-de-lis over other. Two identical tables piled outrageously high with food. GEORGE III *at one.* LOUIS XVI *at other. Gorge yourselves, I mean shove it into your mouths and hold your hands on your mouths to hold it in.* GREEDIES *sing pig song:*

GREEDIES: Dearly beloved brethren,
        Is it not a sin,
        When you peel potatoes,
        To throw away the skins?
        For the skins feed pigs,
        And pigs feed you,
        Dearly beloved brethren,
        Is this not true?

KINGS *throw bones at them.*

LOUIS XVI: Why is it . . .

GEORGE III: . . . everybody who comes within speaking distance . . .

BOTH: . . . wants to wheedle us out of something?

Eat like starved hogs. Say "und" like rooting, voracious hog.

GEORGE III: KARTOFFELSALAT! SCHWANZKOPF! UND, UND, *UND* FLEISCH! UND, UND, *UND* KOPFKÄSE! UND, UND, *UND, UND* KARTOFFELN! UND, *UND, UND, UND,* BLUTWURST!

LOUIS XVI (*say "et" like panting poodle*): GRENOUILLE! CRETIN! ET, ET, *ET, ET* ESCARGOT! ET, ET, ET, *ET, ET* BOEUF! ET, *ET, ET* CÔTE DE VEAU! ET, ET, *ET, ET* CHAMPIGNONS! ET, ET, *ET, ET, ET* PECHES! ET, *ET, ET* POMMES! MOUTON! (*To other side:*) Potatoes and pickled pike. The palette of a peasant in a palace.

GEORGE III *throw bones at him.*

GEORGE III: Slimy snails and slimy frogs and slimy eels. Your SLIMY SLOP makes you walk like a woman. You want one of my troopers to give you some good sausage?

LOUIS XVI *throw bones at him.*

LOUIS XVI: We know about your troopers. Half of them are pregnant by the other half!

77

GEORGE III: And your "troopers"? Women in boots and mustaches, and the men stay at home to knit!

LOUIS XVI (*suck your finger adoringly*): At least these are my people. We are French. You are not even English. My people adore me. I am their King.

From audience, a sullen march of WOMEN.

GEORGE III: "My people adore me. I am their King." My English puppies hate me, but I rule them with an iron fist. *That* is how you keep order in the house, frog-eater.

WOMEN *surround* LOUIS XVI *angrily, sing, shout:*

WOMEN: We want bread *now*! (*Pronounce "breahd."*)

LOUIS XVI: Petit peasant, you have a visitor from over the ocean. In his lit-tle book he writes lit-tle love letters for you. And he wraps a bomb in each one! Pet your English puppies now. They'll bite your hand off!

WOMEN *lift him. Angry shouting:*

WOMEN: BREAD! BREAD! BREAD!

GEORGE III: I would not touch him if he had scrofula!

Tenderly, really not comprehending why they do not eat cake:

LOUIS XVI: Mes gens, pourquoi vous ne mangez pas de gâteau?

Bounce him on trampoline and carry him to Paris.

Blackened CHIMNEY SWEEPS *line up as though in street parade.*

78

MAJOR DOMO: Louis XVI surrounded his capital with foreign mercenaries.

ALL: Paine! Paine! Paine!

REPUTATION: Wake up!

PAINE: Oh, my head.

ALL: PAINE! PAINE! PAINE!

PAINE: Give me a drink. Just one to wake me up.

REPUTATION: Watch this! One-old-man triggers off a megaton of hate.

CAPTAIN LAMBESC *enter. Rotational with* MAJOR DOMO*:*

MAJOR DOMO: The German Cavalry Officer, Captain Lambesc.

The Butcher of Paris.

Swaggers through the poor section.

The chimney sweeps crouch before him.

OLD MAN *enter.*

An old man approaches.

He does not see him!

OLD MAN (*intense anger*): You learn to look quick. When they come, you learn to leave the curb and get out in the street. Or they knock you down. *Knock* you right in the mouth! Three years old or ninety. *Knock* you right down! And you *get off* the curb into the street.

MAJOR DOMO: He knocks him down with his sword!

Pause.

Frozen hate!

REPUTATION: In the streets of Paris. WAKE UP! WATCH THIS!

OLD MAN: The world spins around. I am here in space. They won't let me land on the curb. So I got to straddle it. Legs and arms and STOP IT! Change it around so everybody walks: Out in the street. YOUNG! ONES! AND! OLD! ONES! BLACK! ONES! AND! WHITE! ONES! Out in the streets and walk with me!

Attack CAPTAIN LAMBESC *and rip the clothes off his back.*

Storm the Bastille! We SHALL overcome.

REPUTATION: The ancient, crenellated stone is attacked like a tiger ripping silk.

Tug of war with a large rope. PAINE *on one side.* REPUTATION *on other. Gradually, everyone take sides and tug.*

WAKE UP!

PAINE: Oh, Christ, let me be. I want to sleep.

REPUTATION: The world cracks open. Wake up.

Come on. Say your line!

"Wonders are many, but none is more wonderful than . . ." SAY IT!

PAINE: I want to go a-whoring like anybody else.

ALL: GET UP!

PAINE: I'll be so old I can't get it up.

Who would want you?

You'd be surprised.

ALL: WAKE UP!

REPUTATION: Have you forgotten somewhere in London, in Paris, all those wretches starved by the thousands, cauterizing their guts with hot gin, sleeping twelve in a room, working for sixpence a day.

He wants a mistress.

The revolution is your mistress.

PAINE: Let me alone.

Say the lines the writer wrote for you.

REPUTATION (*very quickly*): "Here sits the typewriter with its keys staring at me, ready to sprinkle millions of letters over an acre of paper. My head breaking with Tom Paine's war." He wants to go a-whoring too, but he sips coffee. Drags a cigarette. NOW HE HAS the line for you.

The telephone rings.

Let it!

He has the line for you, Paine.

ALL: SAY IT! WONDERS ARE MANY, BUT NONE IS MORE WONDERFUL THAN . . .

PAINE: Man. And yet . . .

All giggle.

And yet . . .

All giggle.

And yet . . .

REPUTATION: That's it! Come on! More lines! Many more! Say them!

PAINE (*blurt out in one breath*): And yet animals and insect things laugh at such two-legged pomposity.

Cheers.

REPUTATION: Go on! Move it!

PAINE: Now see what miracles insects perform with their royalty. The king becomes the . . . becomes the . . . becomes the . . .

ALL: BREAD AND CAKE QUEEN!

Tug of war ends.

MAJOR DOMO: The termites of Paris march to the bread and cake queen.

REPUTATION: Now write your second book.

ALL: THE RIGHTS OF MAN!

PAINE *and* REPUTATION *write this with large paint brushes on the wall. Lift* BREAD AND CAKE QUEEN *on one's shoulders. She wears enormous cloth. Group under cloth, clawing outward.*

PAINE *and* REPUTATION *rotational:*

Rotational:

The strangest sight in history.

82

Why is it that such vast classes of mankind are called the ignorant mob? They arise as the unavoidable consequences of old governments! By distortedly exalting some men, others are distortedly debased, till the whole is out of nature. A vast mass of mankind is degraded in the human picture to bring forth with greater glare, the puppet show of state and aristocracy. The mob learns to punish from the governments they live under, and retaliate the punishments they have been accustomed to behold. It signifies nothing to a man what is done to him after he is dead, but it signifies much to the living. It hardens their hearts and instructs them how to punish when power falls into their hands. LAY THE AXE TO THE ROOT,

There is vice in the weather today.

RAIN!!

A droning deluge of rain across the hot July fields.

Nine miles to Versailles.

RAIN!!

The termite queen bloats on eggs. She's the size of a skyscraper.

Stuffed with eggs.

Rain! March in the rain!

The stuff of love bloats her gut.

Lick her sides. Salivate to lubricate,
One hundred-billion eggs of state.

The will of the termites!

ILS VEULENT!

Feed her tiny orifice of taste,
And lick away the eggs of state.

The land is barren of bread and cake,

AND TEACH GOVERN-
MENTS HUMANITY! It
is their sanguinary punishments which corrupt man-
kind. Their hanging, their
drawing and quartering,
tearing to pieces by horses!
Who does not remember
them? This is an age of
revolutions in which everything may be looked for.
All false governments are
military. War is their trade,
plunder and revenue their
objects. The history of these
governments is a disgustful
picture of human wretched-
ness. Wearied with war, and
tired with human butch-
ery . . .

To feed the termite queen
of state.

The termite women march!

In the *driving rain*!

Hungry. Angry.

Eight thousand midwives
march the steamy July
fields.

To Versailles!

To lick the enormous
queen,
To lick the mother-bearer
clean.

Of eggs!

Their staff of life!

THEIR BREAD!

BREAD!!

(Childbearing shriek:)

EAT! CAKE!

The eggs are finished. She
has no more to give. And
yet . . .

(All giggle.)

And yet . . .

(All giggle.)

And yet . . .

(All giggle.)

They continue to lick her
. . . to death.

Dialogues end together. Pause.

ALL: . . . they sit down to rest. And call it peace.

(Sing:)
Tom Paine talked of here and now,
Why should one man's stomach growl,
(Talk:)
And another man say, "You work and slave,
and I'll eat the bread!"

(Sing:)
Why should one man in a palace reside,
(Talk:)
And another man live in a wallow!
(Sing:)
Sometimes living side by side.
Sometimes living side by side.

Mary talks of other things,
The genocide of despotic kings,
(Talk:)
An old man's calumny,
And Frankenstein's monstery
(Sing:)
Tom Paine talked of here and now,
Why should one man's stomach growl?

MARY W.:   His brain aches. He goes to soak it. In
warm gin.

Said Mary Wollstonecraft.

REPUTATION: Put down your bottle. Your brain's pickled.

BLAKE: A suckled red cherry.

Said the mystic Blake.

REPUTATION: You hallucinate on genocide . . .

BLAKE & MARY W.: . . . of a gaggle of kings.

PAINE: The book planted in London, in Bristol, in Edinburgh, in Dublin, even in London Tower his soldiers
read it. This is here and now. Hallucinations don't
carry pistols. His island is honeycombed. Wherever
he walks, the ground gives way under him from
Hebrides to Land's End. He shakes like a toy rattle.

PAINE *drink and fondle the orb*. REPUTATION *throw
it away.*

REPUTATION: Let loose the King from your head. He is
a madman with a crown.

PAINE: I don't want *HIM*!

BLAKE & MARY W.: What do you want?

Litany:

BLAKE: What do you want. From Hebrides to Land's
End?

PAINE: I don't know.

BLAKE & MARY W.: We suspicion.

PAINE: I don't know.

BLAKE & MARY W.: We suspicion.

BLAKE: I see a whale drinking your soul away.

ALL: We suspicion.

MARY W.: My daughter, unborn and gestating, will dwell on Frankenstein's monster, running in the forests silent and gigantic with cataracts FOR EYES!

REPUTATION: What are you conjuring?!

BLAKE & MARY W.: The shadow of Cromwell.

SHADOW: I want . . .

PAINE: I want . . .

BLAKE & MARY W.: We suspicion.

SHADOW: The Hebrides to Land's End.

PAINE: *'TIS A LIE!*

SHADOW: Ye brother crows,
       Take warning all,
       As ye rise,
       So must ye fall.

PAINE: My brain aches.

BLAKE: A suckled red cherry.

REPUTATION: OH, GOD 'TIS A LIE!

BLAKE: Soldiers of the king!

MARY W.: The channel boat. Dover to Calais.

BLAKE: Things in rustling scales rush into reptile coverts.

PAINE: The Rights of Man go with us!

   Exit to cheering group in France. Put tricolor cock-

ade in his hat. Two, hold flags either side of stage,
French and English. Immediately lights.

MAJOR DOMO: Do let us pause and cool the stage for the trial in absentia. The puppet show of state and aristocracy.

Bow, present yourselves:

Barrister Horsely.

ALL: HEAR! HEAR!

MAJOR DOMO: Barrister Edmund Burke.

ALL: HEAR! HEAR!

MAJOR DOMO: The Lord Justice!

ALL: HEAR! HEAR!

LORD JUSTICE: Damn noisy in here.

MAJOR DOMO (*with fervor*): OYEZ! OYEZ! Lord Justice of the Court of the King's Bench. Guildhall, London. December 18, 1792. God bless the King! Shatter his enemies and make them fall! Confound their politics! *Frustrate their knavish tricks. . . .*

LORD JUSTICE: Aren't you getting carried away?

HORSELY: American accents rattle on the eardrum so.

MAJOR DOMO: The Lord Justice opens the trial for libelous passages in the book called *The Rights of Man.*

LORD JUSTICE: Now, gentlemen, his latest book is a unique case. This time he is messing about with our laws.

HORSELY: The laws are already confused enough without him mucking about.

BURKE: Of course. They were written that way for a purpose. For the people's sake.

LORD JUSTICE: Precisely. If you can't convince them. What do you do?

BURKE: Confuse them.

Stamp BURKE's *forehead with big, black rubber stamp.*

JUSTICE & HORSELY: Right.

LORD JUSTICE: A basic principle of law and order.

HORSELY: I don't know what the mass of people in any country have to do with the laws. Except to obey them.

MAJOR DOMO: The Lords temporal said:

Stamp HORSELY.

JUSTICE & BURKE: RIGHT.

HORSELY: *They* are noted for their monosyllables.

BURKE: Paine is a robustious anarchist who is for tearing everything up by the roots, for prostrating government by violence and inflicting upon a nation the heaviest calamities.

HORSELY: *He* is noted for his polysyllables.

LORD JUSTICE: Well now, it is a clear-cut case. It's either yes or no. No or yes. And when you line up the Yesses and the Noseses in some kind of order, except when it's sometimes, of course, *littered* with Maybes and Perhapseses, then you line *all those up* and you take your choice of the various Yesseses and Noseses, the Maybes and the Perhapseses and ah . . . OH! You leave it at that!

ALL THREE: Ahhh, the divine mysteries of the law.

HORSELY: That settles that.

BURKE: However. . . .

HORSELY: Now you're going to confuse it, I know.

BURKE: It's not *really* a Perhapseses, as we understand it, by established precedent.

HORSELY: Didn't I tell you?

BURKE: As in the case of the Crown versus . . .

Stamp BURKE.

JUSTICE & HORSELY: WRONG.

HORSELY: That case was clear-cut. Clear as crystal. A *straightforward* case: of Maybe.

BURKE: Ahhhhh, yes, yes.

LORD JUSTICE: No, no, not Yesseses!

BURKE (*obsequiously*): Oh, Noseses, my Lord.

HORSELY: No, no! It wasn't Noseses! It was MAYBESES! (*Softly:*) Am I right?

Stamp HORSELY.

JUSTICE & BURKE: WRONG.

90

LORD JUSTICE: Or was it? Now that I think about it, maybe it was a case of Noseses. Yesseses! It was Noseses.

Stamp LORD JUSTICE.

BURKE & HORSELY: RIGHT.

LORD JUSTICE (*acidly*): Thank you.

BURKE: It is a difficult decision.

ALL: IT IS a difficult decision.

HORSELY: They're always difficult. Decisions!

LORD JUSTICE: Decisionseses!

BURKE: My lords, it's the only way. Let's flip for it.

LORD JUSTICE: Brilliant man!

HORSELY: A pillar of the Empire!

LORD JUSTICE: An ornament!

Try to one-up each other. End hitting each other.

HORSELY: A sparkling jewel!

LORD JUSTICE: A BREATH OF AIR!

HORSELY: A SILVER TONGUE!

LORD JUSTICE: TWO TURTLE DOVES!

HORSELY: THREE FRENCH HENS!

ALL THREE (*sing*): FIVE GOLDEN RINGS!
        Three French hens,
        Two turtle doves,
        And a partridge in a pear tree. (*Pause.*)
        Ahhhhh, lovely the mysteries of the law.

BURKE: Shall we? Ready then.

LORD JUSTICE: What we won't do for justice.

HORSELY: Do the people really appreciate it?

LORD JUSTICE: My lords, FLIP!

On your heads.

BURKE: Now it's clear as day.

HORSELY: It's so obvious.

LORD JUSTICE: Why didn't we think of it before?

PAINE: My lords.

ALL THREE: Sssssh! We are probing the mysteries of the law.

LORD JUSTICE: My lords, have you touched the mysteries?

BURKE & HORSELY: We have. GUILTY!

LORD JUSTICE: Gentlemen, UNflip.

You do.

Call in the prisoner.

REPUTATION *forward. Indicating* PAINE *on French side.*

BURKE: He's drunk.

PAINE: I'm drunk and you're crazy. Tomorrow I'll be sober, but you'll be crazy the rest of your life.

HORSELY: Sharp-tongued beast, isn't he?

LORD JUSTICE: Well now, Mr. Paine, you have been a busy lit-tle man since you arrived, haven't you?

BURKE: You, at your lit-tle table, with your lit-tle penny pot of ink, hmmmmm?

HORSELY: How did you do it, Mr. Paine? Saaaaavvve it up? Hmmmm? A ha'penny at a time, and put the two together, and trot to the stationers, giggling to yourself.

BURKE: Put down your penny on the counter and say:

LORD JUSTICE: A penny pot of ink, please. I'm going to topple an empire.

BURKE: Is that how it's done?

HORSELY: Make the Lords temporal and the Lords spiritual quake before your lit-tle penny pot of ink?

BURKE: This prodigy of human intellect, this product of ever-renewed intoxication, this leader of the sanguinary rabble of France whose hands are clotted with blood. He staggers under a LOAD OF RUM! Sneaking off to France.

LORD JUSTICE: Since Paine has fled from England . . .

BURKE: The coward.

HORSELY: The spoilsport.

REPUTATION *forward*.

LORD JUSTICE: We will condemn this shadow of him.

ALL: In high absentia.

BURKE: It's a clear-cut case of Yesseses.

LORD JUSTICE: Let's not get started on that again, or we'll be flipping all day.

93

Pause.

Mr. Paine, impartial justice has weighed you in its blindfolded scales and found you wanting.

REPUTATION: I have written the truth. *The Rights of Man* will do for Europe what *Common Sense* has done for America.

LORD JUSTICE: And what, pray tell us, is that beside blood and war?

PAINE: To defend the right of all men to choose their own rulers, to make their own governments, and to get rid of those rulers if they choose.

BURKE: The English people utterly disclaim such a right, and they will resist the assertion with their lives.

REPUTATION: That men should take up arms and spend their lives to maintain they have no rights is a new species of discovery suited to the paradoxical genius of Mr. Burke.

Quacking, honking, gaggle:

ALL THREE: GUILTY! GUILTY! GUILTY!

LORD JUSTICE: You never imagined we'd countenance a revolution. Really, Mr. Paine, we are British, you know.

BURKE: He will cover England with human gore!

BURKE: Look at France!

HORSELY: Sure, look at her.

LORD JUSTICE: Yes, yes, they're worse than we are.

BURKE: Now, what shall we do with him?

HORSELY: Burn him at the stake!

LORD JUSTICE: We can't start a fire on stage.

HORELY: We will put him down!

Do so.

BURKE: And we will blacken his reputation.

LORD JUSTICE: He has fled to France!

Stamp REPUTATION.

ALL: RIGHT!

HORSELY: He stirs up trouble there!

ALL: RIGHT!

BURKE: He plots with Condorcet and the Rabble!

ALL: RIGHT!

LORD JUSTICE: King Louis' sacred person is holed up!

BURKE & HORSELY: WRONG!

HORSELY: He's not holed up. He's still in a palace of 2,000 rooms.

LORD JUSTICE: And not one toilet!

BURKE: The French don't need such things. They use perfume.

JUSTICE & HORSELY: Oh.

BURKE: He called us frauds.

HORSELY: He called us corrupt.

Quickly stamp REPUTATION *all over angrily.*

LORD JUSTICE: Well, there he sits, a mass of contradictions.

ALL: Ahhh, the divine mysteries of the law.

Pause a beat. Now, an unnerving, grinding sound of butcher knife honing. Quick, nervous scurrying, whispers, tocks of wood on wood. ALL *whisper, "Quick."*

REPUTATION: Events rush. Quick! Paris. Quick! Quick! Explosive. Words of petrol. Nod of the head. Death! QUICK! The guillotine. Flash. Explosive. Quick! QUICK! Explosive. Finger itches. QUICK! To strike the match. The king sweats his life. QUICK! QUICK! He cries. QUICK! Pisses himself. Fear. QUICK! Fear. Explosive. QUICK! PARIS. 1793. THE CONVENTION DECIDES IF LOUIS WILL LIVE OR IF HE WILL DIE. THE COMMITTEE OF THE CONVENTION:

Grinding louder. Roll call rotational.

BRISSOT!

VERGNIAUD!

GENSONNÉ!

BARÈRE!

VILLENEUVE!

CONDORCET!

DANTON!

SIEYÈS!

PAINE!

Pound, roar:

KILL THE KING!

Dead quiet. LOUIS *weep in center. Begin as* PAINE *begins: grinding, catcalls, yells.*

PAINE (*breathless rapidity*): Kings have trained the human race to blood. The people must not follow the example by vengeance. Save his life.

Dead quiet. LOUIS *weeps.* ALL *begin again:*

France is the first to abolish kings. Let her be the first to abolish the death vengeance. Save his life.

Dead quiet. LOUIS *weeps.* ALL *begin again:*

Could I speak the French language I would descend to your bar. In your language, beg you not to sever his head.

Dead quiet. LOUIS *weeps.* ALL *begin again:*

Guard him. Detain him until the war ends. Send him in perpetual banishment to America. Save him!

Dead quiet. LOUIS *weeps.*

Save the king!

ALL: *KILL THE KING!*

A great noise. Light man, do brilliant things. LOUIS *carried off.*

Now, a single light on PAINE *only.*

97

PAINE: The Committee of the Convention? Marie? Marie, where are they now? Brissot.

ALL: Guillotined.

PAINE: Vergniaud.

ALL: Guillotined.

PAINE: Gensonné?

ALL: Guillotined.

PAINE: Barère?

ALL: Guillotined.

PAINE: *Villeneuve?!*

ALL: Eaten by wolves.

PAINE: CONDORCET?

ALL: Suicide.

PAINE (*softly*): Danton.

ALL: Guillotined.

PAINE (*very softly*): Sieyès?

MARIE: Everyone died,
    Except Sieyès,
    And he changed sides.

REPUTATION: And except Paine, who was lucky. If you can call it that. He rots in Luxembourg's dungeons and waits for the glittering knife to lift above his neck. The cross of chalk is the signal!

Large iron grill center stage slams down. PAINE *circles like a rat in a maze. Hysterical lifting and*

98

slamming down a stool with hypnotic compulsion.

PAINE, *say roller coaster fast:*

PAINE: The iron cage shut. It swings in and out. Up and down. Locked. SLAM! LOCK! CROSS OF CHALK! STOP!! STOP!!! Iron cage. Swings in. OUT!! Sometimes swings out. OUT!!! Cross of chalk on the door. MARK! BASTARD!! BASTARD, SWING OUT!! Oh, please, BASTARD! IN! OUT!! Oh, Christ, it's shut. IRON SHUT!!! Oh, fuck. Oh, Christ! A jail. CAGE!! THE KNIFE!! I know why I'm here. I KNOW!! Cross of chalk. Oh, iron. IRON!! Oh, Christ, the knife. IT'S SHARP! The bastard. The FUCKING BASTARD! SHARP!! BANG! On my neck. Chink it up. CHINK!! Chink. Chink. Chink a chain up. SLAM!! BANG! DOWN! BANG! On my neck, oh, Christ, dirty bastard. IRON!! SHARP!!! Chink it up again. Chink, chink, chink, chink a chain up. OH, CHRIST! HELP! HOLD IT!!!! Neck down. A block. BASTARD, LAUGH!! Wait. WAIT!!! HOLD IT! STOP!!! Oh, God, here it comes. CLOSE YOUR EYES!!! BITE YOUR TEETH!!! Up and down. Iron. SHARP! Oh, my, wait, wait, wait, wait. HERE IT COMES!!!! It's heavy. Oh, Christ it's heavy. Scaffold trembles. BANG!! SHARP!!! Oh, my neck, it hurts. Wait. CHRIST, HOLD IT!!! Iron. SHARP!! Here it comes. HERE IT COMES!!!! Iron cage. OPEN! Swing out. Goes in. Must go out. OUT!!! OUT!!! BASTARD!!! Oh, God, it's clean. THEY CLEANED IT!!! Help. CHUNK! HERE IT COMES!!! Don't look up. Down. Down. DOWN!! CLOSE YOUR EYES!!

99

Oh, Christ, help. MOVE! CAN'T MOVE! Ears. Please. Please. Please. NOT MY EARS!!! Make a fist. Shut your eyes. Hold your breath. BITE YOUR TEETH!! HERE IT COMES!! WHOOSEH! HERE IT COMES!!! WHOOSEH!! HERE IT COMES!!! HELP! OH GOD! JESUS CHRIST! DON'T LOOK UP!! DOWN! DOWN!! DOWN!!! DOWN!!!! WHOOSEH HERE IT COMES!!!!

ALL: CHUNK!

REPUTATION (*flatly*): One hundred and sixty-eight people are taken out of the Luxembourg each night. One hundred and sixty of them are guillotined the next day. The signal is a cross of chalk on the door of those chosen. For the next day. The guards wait until night. When the prisoners sleep. To mark the signal. So there will be: No panic. In their department. Everyone waits.

One, mark a large cross of chalk. Hang it on the grate.

The prisoners learn self-control. It has been known, in a room full of people, one will start to cry. Then a second. Then a third. Another. And soon, the whole room will cry, silently.

Rotational:

How do you bury a severed body?

Do they bury the head with it?

Do they place the head on the chest? In the hands?

On the neck? Between the legs?

100

Do they put the right head with the right body?

Does it matter?

Do they dig separate graves?

Do they make a trench?

Does it matter?

Where are they all buried?

Does *anyone* know?

Does it make a *difference* to know?

SIMONNE: My name is Simonne. My hair is brown. My eyes are blue. My skin is soft, and in summer it turns brown when it's hot. And in summer, in Lyons, where I live, I walk in the fields. The fields near Lyons have yellow flowers. I walk there in summer, when it's hot, with Jean-Jacques. And our skin turns brown. Together. I want to know. *I* hope it is a field of yellow flowers. I hope . . . please, Bon Dieu . . . let it be.

SIMONNE *weeps. Then* ALL.

REPUTATION: Then a second. Then a third. Another. And soon. All.

Guitar music start.

MAJOR DOMO: A curious twist of fate, the cross of chalk on the iron plate was turned around and the avenging angel passed him by. The world flies through space attracting meteors. Notre Dame, the great cathedral, is now a dance hall. A clean sweep has made even the calendar obey. And the revolution

101

supplants Jesus as the reckoning day. So it is the Year One. The earth is as pure again as when Adam said "Begin." Madame Bonville teaches Monsieur Paine the new calendar at Number 4, rue du Théâtre Français.

ALL: And it's September in a kissproof world.

MARGUERITE: The days of the month are thirty. The months of the year are twelve. What passes in between can be whatever you want it to be. It's simple.

PAINE *speak English*. MARGUERITE *sing French*.

September.
Vendémiaire.
The month of grapes.
Le mois vendange.

October.
Brumaire.
The month of mists.
Le mois brumeux.

November.
Frimaire.
The freezing month.
Le mois des vents froids.

December.
Nivose.
The month of snow.
Le mois neigeux.

January.
Pluviose.

The month of rains.
Le mois pluvieux.

February.
Ventose.
The month of winds.
Le mois éventé.

March.
Germinal.
The month of seeds.
Le mois des semences.

April.
Floreal.
The month of flowers.
Le mois fleuri.

May.
Prairial.
The pastoral month.
Le mois champêtre.

June.
Messidor.
The good month.
Le mois du bien-être.

July.
Thermidor.
The hot month.
Le mois des grandes chaleurs.

August.
Fructidor.
The month of fruitful things.
Le mois des fruits.

MAJOR DOMO: That year, Thomas Paine Bonville was born. Some say the child was his. Some say not. Marguerite only smiled. It's a thing called style.

MARGUERITE: And then what did you do?

PAINE: Then? Old and sick from the prison. I try to remember. I lay in bed. I try to remember, but the more I try . . .

MARIE: Then you went back to New York.

PAINE: To the bear pit.

MARGUERITE: No, not yet. You went back to New York. I went with you.

PAINE: Can't remember. Give me a drink, please. Please . . . Marie.

REPUTATION: You went back to your farmhouse alone. And the mob taunted you. And they threw rocks at your windows. And the toughs baited you. And they pushed you in the mud.

Rotational:

Damned if he'll sleep in the same barn with us.

Filthy creep.

He denied God in his black book.

PAINE: The Age of Reason does not deny God.

Rotational:

It says religion is set up for plunder and profit. If that don't deny God, what does?

And it gets worse page by page.

And the country you named, ganged up.

Push, shove, taunt him. ALL *chant street jargon:*

Make a revolution, blood and flame,
I'm the one who does it. My name is Paine.
I should have gone to the guillotine,
AND LET THE KNIFE CHOP OFF YOUR
LYING HEAD
TO LEARN VARIOUS AND ASSORTED
OTHER
PERSONAGES WHO MURDER AND ARE
INCENDIARIES AND REVOLUTIONISTS
AND WHO OUR
GREAT SOCIETY DISLIKES TO PUT UP
WITH!

PAINE: MARIE! MARIE, then I went to the bear pit to be left in peace?!

MARIE: You went to your farmhouse. Alone. You lit the fire at night, and the drums and the fifes crackled and licked at your memory, marching feet of comrades all gone.

Rotational:

Paine we need guns.

Paine we need powder.

Cannon, shot and more than balls.

We need meat.

We'll settle for hardtack.

We need boots.

We can't fight the damned war on good intentions.

ONE: Paine the quartermaster blames the paymaster.

ONE & TWO: The paymaster blames the generals.

ONE, TWO & THREE: The generals blame the congress.

ONE, TWO, THREE & FOUR: The congress blames the traitors.

ALL: AND THE TRAITORS SAY, GET STUFFED!

PAINE: Leave me alone! Marie, let me go to the bear pit. NOW?!

MARIE: You went to vote.

PAINE: Oh, Christ, give me a drink!

MARGUERITE: Then what happened?

REPUTATION: You went to vote. You left the farmhouse. You walked to town. In the nation you named. In the nation you made. Four million people are your credentials. You stand in line. There is a table. The registrars sit before it. They smile. They stroke their noses. They narrow their eyes. They smile. They look at each other. They smile. They look at you.

Each REGISTRAR *on someone's shoulders. Large black robes to floor cover them. Each wears a peruke.*

REGISTRAR 1: Your name?

REPUTATION: They look at your fierce hooked nose. Your twisted eyes. Your filth. Your rumpled clothes.

PAINE: My name?! My name is Thomas Paine.

106

REGISTRAR 1: Do be serious. Voting is serious business.

REGISTRAR 2: This trembling old man is the thundering revolutionist?

REGISTRAR 1: Absurd.

PAINE: I want to register.

REGISTRAR 1: Indeed.

REGISTRAR 2: I'm afraid you cannot vote.

REGISTRAR 1: You are not a citizen.

REGISTRAR 2: You are a foreigner.

REGISTRAR 1: You are not a citizen of the United States.

PAINE: I am Thomas Paine. I have given the name to this country which I have come to love above all else. I have spent my life forging its principles and spreading those principles to the world.

REGISTRAR 2: Yes, yes, that's splendid, but can you prove you are a citizen?

REGISTRAR 1: Were you ever formally made a citizen?

PAINE: Formalities? No, no, my life has been spent breaking down formalities.

REGISTRAR 2: Ah, then you are still English.

MARIE: He can't return to England. They'll hang him on sight.

REGISTRAR 1: So we understand.

REGISTRAR 2: Then you cannot vote anywhere.

REGISTRAR 1: You are an alien.

REGISTRAR 2: A refugee.

REGISTRAR 1: You really have no country, Mr. Paine.

PAINE: BUT I HAVE THE RIGHT TO VOTE!!

REGISTRAR 2: YOU HAVE NO RIGHTS AT ALL, DRUNKEN FOOL! DO YOU WANT TO GO TO PRISON?!

PAINE: No . . . not prison again. But I am Thomas Paine, returned home to the country I love and fought for.

Laughter.

REGISTRAR 1: We do not register foreigners.

REGISTRAR 2: You are not a citizen.

REGISTRAR 1: You cannot vote.

REGISTRAR 2: You are holding up the line.

REGISTRAR 1: Move on, old man.

Laughter.

PAINE: What am I to do now? Marie, MARIE, THE BEAR PIT, NOW?!

MARIE: Now it is the time for that.

PAINE: Give me a drink.

REPUTATION: First the bear pit. Then the sickness. And then you lay a-dying and the swarms of do-good-greedies flocked about to catch the plum of converting the great Paine back to the fold.

A heartbeat, steady and rhythmic, louder and louder and quicker and quicker.

108

DO-GOOD-GREEDIES' *rotational:*

Mr. Paine, do you wish to ask God's forgiveness?

Mr. Paine, do you want to recant?

Mr. Paine, do you hear me?

Mr. Paine, do you still persist in heresy?

From here, start to emerge from characters back to yourselves as indicated; and at varying times.

ACTOR OF REPUTATION: Oh, they put a bad mouth on him and hacked him up and they did him most bad. And there wasn't a mother who would waste spit on him. (*To* SERGEANT:) And what can he do now? Well, his heart will break open. And it will float away.

SERGEANT: Whaaaaat? Oh, come on, cut the theatrical nonsense.

PRIVATE: Tell the story straight.

ACTOR OF REPUTATION: And his heart broke open. And it floated away in the air.

SERGEANT: Hey. HEY! Come on, wake up! I got my orders to bring him in. HEY, YOU! HEY, CUT THAT OUT!

Heartbeat reaches a peak and stops. Red balloons fly out from him and float over the entire audience to the ceiling.

ACTOR OF REPUTATION: Now you did it.

ACTOR OF MAJOR DOMO: Poor old drunk.

ACTRESS OF MARIE: Well, Sergeant, did the second act help you?

SERGEANT: What's the matter with you people? Can't anybody tell a straight story any more? I asked for Tom Paine, not this beggar you created.

ACTRESS OF MARIE: We tried, [use name of actor].

ACTOR OF MAJOR DOMO: Let's say he was ahead of his time for his country. And the way things look, he's getting farther and farther ahead.

ACTOR OF SERGEANT: Well, did he want to be a king, or didn't he?!

ACTOR OF GEORGE III: That's an easy way to explain him away.

ACTOR OF REPUTATION: IT'S A COP-OUT!

ACTOR OF LOUIS XVI: Well, that's the end. There's no more script left.

Rotational:

Anybody seen the drum?

It's on my hump, over by [use name of actress].

Come on, let's get these props off-stage.

Who's going for coffee?!

Oh, give us some music to end this or we'll all leave sad.

Start to straggle off singing "Tom Paine came from

110

*afar, afar." It grows and grows, louder and louder
with drums, gongs, and noises.*

What about him?

He'll sober up.

One of the turtles escaped.

Switch off the light board.

Put the turtles in the water tank.

One of them escaped!

More animals in this show.

Nasally, mocking a bad line:

If there were three acts . . .
. . . we'd have elephants.

Light fading, and music growing louder and louder.

ACTOR OF PAINE: And the raw stuff, the raw stuff that
moved the pen was dumped into a hole in an empty
field. Then, Marie, one last act of revenge. In the
night, they invaded the farm and they hacked the
trees and ripped up the few flowers and with iron
hammers they broke the stone above his head, and
dug up his very bones and they shoveled them into
a sack and they threw them aboard a ship bound
for London to hang upside down before the jeering
mobs. And when they were done, the bones, the
raw stuff that moved the pen, were thrown into the
street. And nobody knows where they are today. So
went Tom Paine who shook continents awake. And
today, right now, his small statue is splashed in red

paint in a small farm in a small town in a nation growing smaller and smaller (*light fading*) and smaller and smaller and smaller. (*And the music growing louder and louder and louder and louder.*)

CURTAIN

PAINE! PAINE!

Music by Tom O'Horgan

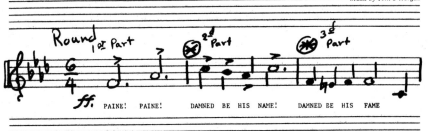

PAINE! PAINE! DAMNED BE HIS NAME! DAMNED BE HIS FAME

AND LASTING HIS SHAME! GOD DAMN PAINE! GOD DAMN PAINE!

GIN! GIN! GIN!

— *Music by Tom O'Horgan*

Look a - round Lon - don what do you see? Age to the poor - house, youth to the gal - lows. Be-cause of ... GIN! GIN! GIN! E - nough to float the na - vy in. GIN! GIN! GIN! It's good for ev -ery-thing. GIN! GIN! GIN! Sores and pock holes, run - ny wham holes. GIN! GIN! GIN! WASH THE BABIES IN IT! GIN! GIN! GIN! THE GUT-TERS RUN WITH IT! GIN! GIN! GIN!

IF YOU'RE NOT BLOOD IN ENGLAND

Music by Tom O'Horgan

If you're not blood in Eng-land,

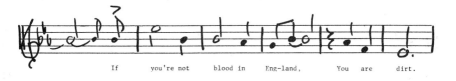

If you're not blood in Eng-land, You are dirt.

You are dirt. For dirt in England, Dirt

breeds dirt.

TOM PAINE CAME FROM AFAR, AFAR

———Music by Tom O'Horgan

Tom Paine came from a-far, a-far, His nose is like a blaz-ing star. He stirred the world a-

round and round, And turned the hea - vens

up - side down.

rit

BLACK DICK

—Music by Tom O'Horgan

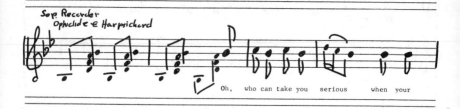

Sop. Recorder
Ophiclide & Harpsichord

Oh, who can take you serious when your

name is Black Dick, when your name is Black Dick. Oh, who can take you

serious when your name is Black Dick.

Solo

When

All

brains	were	passed	around the	floor,	Black	Dick stood be-hind the door. But
put	their	money	on	his nose.	Black	Dick stood and there he froze.
bet	that he	would	rise and	shine.	Black	Dick's horse was left be-hind.
-bility		is	bound to	rise.	Why	should it come as a surprize.

JIM CROW

— *Music by Tom O'Horgan*

girls wANk!. wANk!. wANk!. wANk!. **Boys (Falsetto)** Here lies the body of Jim Crow, who was high but

now is low. Ye broth-er crows take warn-ing all. For as ye rise, so

must ye fall. For as ye rise so must ye fall.

THE GREEDIES' SONG

Music by Tom O'Horgan

Dear-ly be-lov-ed breth — ren, Is it not a sin, When

you peel po — ta-toes, To throw a-way the skins?

For the skins feed pigs, And pigs feed you.

Dear-ly be-lov-ed breth — ren. Is this not true?

TOM PAINE TALKED OF HERE AND NOW

— Music by Tom O'Horgan

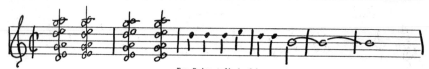

Tom Paine talked of here and now,

Why should one man's stom-ach growl,
(SPOKEN) And another man say, "You work and slave,
and I'll eat the bread"!

Why should one man in a pal-ace re – side,
(SPOKEN) And another man live in a wallow!

Some-times liv – ing side by side.
(SPOKEN) Sometimes living side by side.

Ma – ry talks of oth-er things.
(SPOKEN) Mary talks of other things.

The

gen-o-cide   of   des-   potic   kings,
                    (SPOKEN) An old man's calumny,
                    And Frankenstein's monstery.

Tom   Paine talked of   here and   now,

Why   should   one man's   stom-ach   grrrrowl?

THE REVOLUTIONARY CALENDAR

Music by Tom O'Horgan

Le mois des vents froids. *hum* — Le mois neigeux. *hum* — Le

(PAINE) The freezing month. December. The month of snow. January.

(MARGUERITE) Nivose. (MARGUERITE) Pluviose.

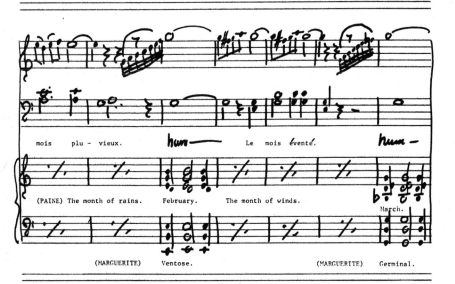

mois plu - vieux. *hum* — Le mois éventé. *hum* —

(PAINE) The month of rains. February. The month of winds.

March.

(MARGUERITE) Ventose. (MARGUERITE) Germinal.

Le mois des se – men-ces.   hum —   Le mois fleur - i.   hum —

(PAINE) The month of seeds.   April.   The month of flowers.   May.

(MARGUERITE)   Floreal.   (MARGUERITE)   Prairial.

Le mois champêtre.   hum —   Le mois du bien-être.   hum —

(PAINE) The pastoral month.   June.   The good month.   July.

(MARGUERITE)   Messidor.   (MARGUERITE)   Thermidor.

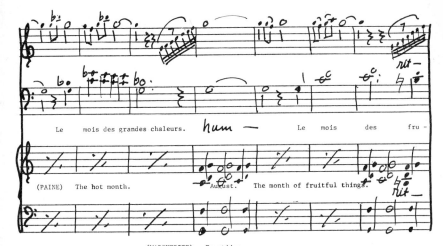

Le mois des grandes chaleurs. hum — Le mois des fru -

(PAINE) The hot month. August. The month of fruitful things.

(MARGUERITE) Fructidor.

its.